The

QUALITY

Infrastructure

ALA Editions purchases fund advocacy, awareness,
and accreditation programs for library professionals worldwide.

The
QUALITY
Infrastructure

Measuring, Analyzing, and Improving Library Services

Edited by

SARAH ANNE MURPHY

AMERICAN LIBRARY ASSOCIATION
CHICAGO 2014

SARAH ANNE MURPHY has held numerous positions at the Ohio State University Libraries since 1999. She is currently coordinator of assessment there. Murphy earned an MLS degree from Kent State University in 2000 and an MBA from Ohio State's Fisher College of Business in 2008. She is author of *The Librarian as Information Consultant* (2011), and has published papers on Lean Six Sigma, mentoring, and issues related to veterinary medicine libraries in *College & Research Libraries,* the *Journal of Academic Librarianship,* and the *Journal of the Medical Library Association.*

© 2014 by the American Library Association

Printed in the United States of America

18 17 16 15 14   5 4 3 2 1

Extensive effort has gone into ensuring the reliability of the information in this book; however, the publisher makes no warranty express or implied, with respect to the material contained herein.

ISBNs: 978-0-8389-1173-0 (paper); 978-0-8389-9496-2 (PDF); 978-0-8389-9495-5 (ePub); 978-0-8389-9497-9 (Kindle). For more information on digital formats, visit the ALA Store at alastore.ala.org and select eEditions.

Library of Congress Cataloging-in-Publication Data

The quality infrastructure : measuring, analyzing, and improving library services / edited by Sarah Anne Murphy.
       pages cm
    Includes bibliographical references and index.
    ISBN 978-0-8389-1173-0
       1. Academic libraries—United States—Evaluation—Case studies. 2. Research libraries—United States—Evaluation—Case studies. 3. Public services (Libraries)—Evaluation—Case studies. 4. Libraries—Quality control—Case studies. 5. Library administration—United States—Case studies. 6. Library administration—Canada—Case studies. I. Murphy, Sarah Anne.
    Z675.U5Q35 2014
    025.5'87—dc23   2013005034

Cover design by Adrianna Sutton. Image © Shutterstock, Inc.
Text design in the Chaparral, Gotham, and Bell Gothic typefaces by Karen Sheets de Gracia

♾ This paper meets the requirements of ANSI/NISO Z39.48-1992 (Permanence of Paper).

Contents

Introduction

QUALITY FUNCTIONS AS A STRATEGIC COMPETITIVE ASSET, and libraries with high-functioning quality infrastructures, defined by programs with dedicated personnel, are best positioned to demonstrate their value. This collection of essays, written by authors from a variety of backgrounds and library institutions, is dedicated to promoting the benefits of developing a quality infrastructure within a library organization. By dedicating a department, committee, or employee to assessment activities, or implementing programs such as the Baldrige Criteria for Performance Excellence, Lean Six Sigma, or the Balanced Scorecard, these libraries have realized sustainable change. The contributors to this volume show that it is possible to establish a programmatic approach to measuring, analyzing, and improving library services whether a library serves a large research-intensive university, a small liberal arts college, or is itself a special library. Such discipline not only improves the value of library services, but aids a library or library organization in communicating its value to the individuals it serves.

Our hope is to expand librarians' conversations on assessment beyond specific tools to measure customer perceptions of service quality, learning outcomes, and website usability. While knowledge and application of such tools is necessary to develop an understanding of library customers' needs and a library's success at satisfying these needs, these tools, used in isolation, cannot effect sustainable change. A library can only continuously improve and effectively respond to the needs of the individuals it serves by dedicating the human, financial, and capital resources required to support effective assessment.

These resources are the foundation for any library assessment program. Regardless of whether a library refers to its efforts to understand the effectiveness of its services and programs as assessment, quality improvement, impact evaluation, or evidence-based librarianship, a library with an effective quality infrastructure must invest in the personnel supporting these programs, and provide the equipment and finances necessary to do their work. Further, personnel in such programs ideally follow a process or model for structuring their work. Lean Six Sigma and the Baldrige Criteria, for example, offer a framework that aids an organization's efforts to consistently seek improvement. By working through Lean Six Sigma's Define-Measure-Analyze-Improve-Control (DMAIC) model, or the Baldrige Criteria's structured questions, a library may efficiently gather information regarding a problem or situation and take effective action. Consciously following such processes prevents library employees from skipping important steps in the improvement process, such as failing to truly consider the voice of the customer or understand the root cause of an issue. Further, by using these processes, or tools such as the Balanced Scorecard, library employees are better positioned to effectively work together and communicate their progress to others.[1]

While the implementation of formal assessment or quality infrastructures in libraries is evolving, a variety of approaches are relevant, depending on the size of the institution the library supports, and factors such as the library and the institution's culture. Further, many libraries may have already consciously or unconsciously adopted elements of established quality infrastructures or programs. A recent survey of 536 academic libraries employing more than ten professional librarians and having a Carnegie Foundation Basic Classification of Master's/S or above, for instance, revealed that just five of 158 responding libraries (3.1 percent) utilized Lean Six Sigma or another established quality improvement program to structure or organize their library's assessment program.[2] An additional 36 libraries (22.8 percent), however, indicated that while they had no formally established quality infrastructure, they did have a framework or system for identifying, prioritizing, and organizing assessment projects. While nearly all survey respondents (n = 151, 95.5 percent) indicated that their library leaders promoted and supported the gathering and utilization of assessment or quality improvement data, less than half of the same survey respondents (n = 70, 44.3 percent) indicated that their library provides a budget to support their assessment or quality improvement activities. Only half (n = 83, 52.5 percent) noted their library had staff specifically assigned to coordinate their library's assessment or quality improvement program.

Without devoting a budget or staff to programmatically measuring, analyzing, and improving library services, libraries will continue to struggle to sustain assessment efforts and consistently demonstrate their value. The contributors to this book were tasked to share how a systematic quality or assessment program was established within their library organization, detail the roles established for individuals participating in the program, discuss recent activities or projects, and indicate how their program has affected sustainable change within their organization as evidenced by continuous learning and improvement.

The evolution of the well-respected assessment program at the University of Washington Libraries is outlined by Steve Hiller and Stephanie Wright in chapter 1. The program was established with a task force appointed to study the needs of the libraries' users and the success of the libraries in satisfying these needs in 1991, and activities are now directed by an Office of Assessment and Planning, which diligently works to link assessment with the libraries' strategic planning initiatives using the Balanced Scorecard framework. The office is staffed by a director who serves as an internal consultant for assessment activities conducted by library staff, and a part-time management information librarian, who assists the director in developing, implementing, and managing the program. Two standing committees, the Strategic Planning Action Team and the Libraries Assessment and Metrics Team, support the activities of the office, helping to develop outcomes and success metrics, and making data and other key information available to staff and the public. Ongoing projects include the Triennial and In-Library Use surveys which provide longitudinal information detailing how students and faculty use the libraries and their information needs and priorities. Usability and other qualitative assessment methods are also conducted, and e-metrics focused on electronic resource usage and costs are collected.

The development of the Management Information Services Department at the University of Virginia Libraries is discussed by Lynda White in chapter 2. Formed in 1997, the department is now staffed by three full-time employees dedicated to assessment, data collection, analysis, and reporting. The director researches assessment tools and provides data on demand while the associate director focuses on gathering and analyzing qualitative data, and a programmer provides specialized services for various assessment-related projects. Significant projects include the adaptation of the Balanced Scorecard in 2001 to monitor the overall health of the libraries. Metrics for the scorecard focus on various aspects of the libraries' operations and are reviewed annually to confirm ongoing relevance. Recent initiatives include the administration of a work-life survey designed to gather information on organizational communication issues, employee job satisfaction, staff development, and other issues. The department distributes a user satisfaction survey to approximately one third of the university's population annually, allowing faculty and students to share their opinions regarding the library's collections, services, and facilities.

The University of Arizona Libraries' unique approach to continuously improving collections and services is shared by Chestalene Pintozzi in chapter 3. By adopting core elements of management philosophies, such as Total Quality Management or Six Sigma, and designing their organizational structure around these principles, the libraries has positioned itself to understand the needs and expectations of its primary user groups and stakeholders. Recent projects have resulted in the redeployment of staff at library reference and information desks, cost savings for interlibrary loan through process improvement, and systems for aligning team and personal goals with the libraries' strategic plan. The libraries administers LibQUAL annually to assess service quality in relation to customer expectations. It also distributes a Library Services Survey to determine how well the libraries' Information Commons is meeting user needs. Ongoing challenges for the libraries' assessment and planning initiatives include the identification of appropriate outcome measures, and the efficiency and accuracy of data collection and reporting.

Syracuse University Library's Program Management Center (PMC) is introduced by Terriruth Carrier and Nancy Turner in chapter 4. To proactively demonstrate the library's value, the PMC has adopted aspects of the Six Sigma and Project Management Professional (PMP) approaches to investigation, data collection, analysis, and process improvement. The PMC consists of four full-time employees and includes a director who is a certified Project Management Professional. The director is responsible for developing the library's assessment program, while the head of user research and assessment librarian focuses on studying patron use of library services, facilities, and resources. The application and statistical analyst librarian manages the library's data sets and develops programs that support staff responsible for collecting data, while the project coordinator and data specialist monitors project milestones and also consolidates and analyzes data. Two projects that illustrate the PMC's approach to library assessment are detailed in this chapter: the Gate Count and Security Alarm project, and the Library Measures Data Repository.

An implementation of the Baldrige Criteria for Performance Excellence by the Information Service Office (ISO) at the National Institute of Standards and Technology, as a means to allow ISO to quickly respond to changing technologies and customer expectations, is outlined by Barbara Silcox, Mary-Deirdre Corragio, Susan Makar, and Mylene Ouimette in chapter 5. The ISO uses the Baldrige Criteria to systematically involve its entire workforce in strategic planning and organizational assessment. To showcase role model practices that have enabled the organization to create a culture focused on knowledge sharing, improvement, and results, details of ISO's Lab Liaison Program, Vision Implementation Project, and Workforce Development and Performance Management Systems are provided. Such practices have allowed the organization to maintain its focus on creating value for both customers and key stakeholders.

Another application of the Baldrige Criteria for Performance Excellence is detailed by Xuemao Wang and Emily Thornton of the Emory University Libraries in chapter 6. The historical context for the libraries' decision to adopt the program as a means for guiding self-assessment and continuous improvement is provided along with a review of the libraries' efforts to address the detailed questions included in each of the seven categories of the Baldrige Framework and provide specific examples of the benefits and challenges the libraries realized after applying the criteria. While work in applying the criteria continues, hope remains that the criteria will offer the libraries a means to integrate its performance improvement initiatives and establish an organizational culture driven by excellence.

A consortial perspective is provided by Dana Thomas and Kate Davis through a review of the development of the Ontario Council of University Libraries' (OCUL's) evaluation and assessment program in chapter 7. Focused on supporting OCUL's Scholars Portal suite of information resources and services, the program is influencing the development of both the consortium's and member libraries' collections and services. Notable projects include the development of the Scholars Portal Usage Data utility, which allows consortium members to pull COUNTER-compliant usage data for books and journals accessed through the locally developed Scholars Portal interface. The Serials Collection Overlap Tool also enables both the consortium and member institutions to make informed decisions regarding whether to retain existing or acquire new content by highlighting the number of unique titles that would be added through a purchase, or lost in a cancellation.

The University of California-San Diego Libraries' unique approach to managing the libraries' assessment activities and supporting data-driven decision making is discussed by Kymberly Goodson and Daniel Suchy in chapter 8. Rather than appointing an assessment committee or coordinator, the libraries chose to create and fill four analyst positions: the decision support analyst, the user services technology analyst, the collection services analyst, and the business analyst. The roles and responsibilities for two of these analyst positions, the decision support and user services technology analysts, are specifically outlined in the chapter. Recent activities include ongoing usability testing to redesign and maintain the libraries' website, online tutorials, and locally produced digital collections; assessment of the content of chat, text, and e-mail reference questions; and collection and analysis of data for the libraries' space reconfiguration projects. Projects completed by the decision support analyst have informed the libraries' budget reduction strategies, while projects of the user services technology analyst have directly informed decisions related to adopting potential technologies and services or continuing with current technologies and services.

The responsibilities of the Kansas State University Libraries' Office of Library Planning and Assessment are outlined by Laurel Littrell in chapter 9. Established after a major organizational restructuring in 2010, the office is tasked with increasing assessment capacity to support the libraries' strategic planning efforts and the university's accreditation needs. The office's director is responsible for leading the libraries' strategic planning process, monitoring the implementation of the libraries' strategic plan, and ensuring that the libraries' strategic initiatives remain aligned with the university's strategic agenda. A research and development librarian and a service quality librarian are responsible for studying customer satisfaction and researching new products, services, and practices for implementation throughout the Kansas State University Libraries. A library data coordinator supports office activities by collecting, maintaining, and disseminating statistics related to the libraries' operations. Current activities include supporting the university's re-accreditation bid, introducing a strategic planning process for the libraries in 2012, and administering LibQUAL.

A model for creating an assessment program with limited staff resources in a small liberal arts college setting is shared by Lucretia McCulley of the University of Richmond in chapter 10. The Boatwright Memorial Library's Assessment Committee uses a focused approach to work together as a team to employ a number of assessment tools and methodologies to gather information on student learning, user services, and building facilities. The committee collaborates with other departments on campus, such as the Office of Institutional Effectiveness and the Student Development Division, to maximize resources, inform its work, and successfully execute assessment projects. Further collaborations with the university's Sociology and Anthropology Department has provided valuable feedback on student behavior in their library.

Lastly, a hybrid structure for supporting an assessment program at Washington University in St. Louis is detailed by Carol Mollman in chapter 11. With an Assessment Team led by a full-time assessment coordinator, the libraries has successfully developed a culture of assessment via regular communication forums and by identifying opportunities to involve over 88 percent of all staff in assessment activities. A formal process for initiating, conducting, and completing assessment projects has been established, and projects are supported by specialized subgroups of the Assessment Team. Recent activities include the deployment of an in-house Service Quality Survey, which identified user concerns regarding Wi-Fi coverage within library buildings, the libraries' hours, and the availability of collaborative work areas. While the program is still evolving, Mollman provides structured commentary illustrating how it has served as a catalyst for change.

While the chapters in this book are not intended to be read in any particular order, they do illustrate that establishing a formal infrastructure for supporting a library's quality or assessment program is imperative for the program's success. Many models for these infrastructures exist and may be adapted and applied in academic libraries of various sizes and organizational and political cultures. By establishing a programmatic approach to measuring, analyzing, and improving library services, academic libraries can realize sustainable change and better position themselves to communicate their value.

Sarah Anne Murphy, MLS, MBA
Coordinator of Assessment
Ohio State University Libraries

NOTES

1. Nancy Tague, *The Quality Toolbox*, 2nd ed. (Milwaukee, WI: ASQ Quality, 2005), 35.
2. Sarah A. Murphy, "Quality Frameworks for Academic Libraries: Organizing and Sustaining Library Assessment Activities," Library Assessment Conference, Charlottesville, Virginia, October 31, 2012.

STEVE HILLER AND
STEPHANIE WRIGHT
Office of Assessment and Planning,
University of Washington Libraries

1
From User Needs to Organizational Performance

Twenty Years of Assessment at the
University of Washington Libraries

THE UNIVERSITY OF WASHINGTON (UW) IS A LARGE, COMPRE-
hensive research university with a main campus located in Seattle,
Washington, and two smaller branch campuses within thirty-five miles. The
university has ranked first among public universities in the amount of funding received from federal research awards since the 1970s (second overall) and
is rated among the top twenty-five research universities in the world by the
Times of London and the Academic Ranking of World Universities. Current
student enrollment is approximately 30,000 undergraduate students and
15,000 graduate and professional students.

The University of Washington Libraries' long-established and robust
assessment program has delivered critical information about user needs,
library and information use, importance, impact, and priorities during the
past twenty years. Employing a variety of qualitative and quantitative assessment methods, including a large scale-triennial survey of faculty and students
conducted since 1992, the libraries uses assessment information extensively
in planning, program development, service evaluation, and in communicating the value of the library to the broader community. The UW Libraries

has developed and fostered a "culture of assessment" where evidence-based decision making and a user-centered focus are expectations from line staff to administration. Libraries staff have made substantial contributions to the library assessment field in such areas as user needs assessment, usability, collections and resources usage, space planning, and organizational performance assessment. As cofounder and cosponsor of the biennial Library Assessment Conference, the University of Washington Libraries has been an influential leader in promoting and nurturing the value of assessment for libraries and their communities.

Organizationally, the program has progressed from a committee to a part-time assessment coordinator to an Office of Assessment and Planning, headed by a director who is part of the libraries' administrative leadership. Established in 2006, this office works to integrate assessment with strategic planning utilizing the Balanced Scorecard organizational performance model. Two standing committees, the Strategic Planning Action Team and the Libraries Assessment and Metrics Team, play instrumental roles in supporting these efforts.

This chapter will review the development of assessment efforts at the University of Washington Libraries and the evolution of an assessment program from one that focused primarily on user needs assessment to one that is integrated with planning and organizational performance. More information about the UW Libraries assessment program, including survey forms and results, can be found at the UW Libraries Assessment website.[1]

Program Foundation, 1991–1994

The University of Washington Libraries established a library assessment program in 1991. (See figure 1.1.) The initial catalyst for development arose from the libraries' first strategic plan that year, which called for a user-centered approach to services and resources. Specifically, the plan called for the libraries to "develop and implement a study to identify user populations, their information needs, and how well they are being met."[2] Prior efforts to gain information about user needs were sporadic, narrowly focused, or user-initiated. Indirect cost studies conducted by consultants for the university in the 1980s did include a short survey at campus libraries which gathered basic demographic information and the purpose of the visit (research, teaching/learning, etc.). However, the data were not used by the libraries for assessing user behavior or programmatic change. Similarly, while statistics were available for such areas as circulation and reference, the data had not been analyzed or used for improvement.

FIGURE 1.1

Organizational Infrastructure for Library Assessment 1991–present

Year	Groups	Leadership/Support	Reports to
1991–1997	Task Force on Library Services	Cochairs	Associate Director, Public Services
1997–1999	Library Assessment Group	Chair	Associate Director, Research and Instructional Services
1999–2006	Library Assessment Group	Library Assessment Coordinator (50%)	Associate Dean, Research and Instructional Services
2006–2008	Library Assessment Group	Director, Assessment and Planning Management Information Librarian (50%)	Director, Assessment and Planning
2008–	Libraries Assessment and Metrics Team	Team Chair Director Assessment and Planning Other support (25%)	Director, Assessment and Planning

Betty Bengtson, director of the University Libraries, appointed the Task Force on Library Services in 1991. The task force was charged to develop and implement a study to identify the libraries' various user populations and their needs for library services; to evaluate how well the University Libraries is meeting those needs; to recommend any needed modifications in or additions to the current array of services offered; to recommend levels of library services to be provided to primary and secondary users; and to prepare detailed reports at each phase of study, evaluation, and recommendation.

To achieve these goals, the task force developed a survey that was mailed out in 1992 to faculty and students with the intent to determine who the library users and potential users were, why they used (or didn't use) the library, what resources and services were used, and what their needs for library-related information were. The survey, which later became known as the Triennial Survey, also asked how satisfied faculty and students were with the resources and services of the library. The following year, the task force developed an In-Library Use Survey to gather data about the use of library services by nonaffiliated visitors. These two surveys provided the basis for what was to become a lengthy history of user-centered and evidence-based decision making.

Developing an Ongoing Assessment Program, 1995–1999

The UW Libraries' focus on understanding user needs and ensuring that programs and services addressed those needs were central to the development of a robust assessment program. The user-centered approach to services was also seen as the responsibility of all library staff members. The 1995–1999 Strategic Plan reiterated the commitment to a user-centered library:

> A user-centered services program must be at the heart of the Libraries' activities. User-centered services are the responsibility of all Libraries units. Each unit must understand who its users, or customers, are. Whom do the units serve and what user needs they are trying to meet are the critical questions. Continued attention is required to user needs assessment.[3]

This was translated into the first goal and corresponding objective of the 1995–1999 Strategic Plan: "Enhance and strengthen services based on user needs" and "Implement ongoing user needs assessment and develop criteria to measure quality of service."

The charge for the Task Force on Library Services was revised in 1995 to provide support for the libraries' 1995–99 Strategic Plan as well as to reflect the success of the user surveys. The revised charge asked the task force to build on the spring 1992 faculty and student surveys and conduct faculty and student surveys during spring 1995; finalize a service levels policy and a schedule and plan for implementation; develop criteria to measure the quality of library services; and recommend organizational strategies for ongoing user needs assessment.

As the scope and range of assessment activities increased throughout the libraries, the need for an ongoing, coordinated program of assessment assumed greater importance. The Task Force on Library Services recommended that it be dissolved in 1997 and suggested that an assessment coordinator position be created that would work closely with a new group focused on library assessment. The cover letter to the task force's report noted that

as a result of the Task Force's work, the Libraries now has a service policy and valuable information on the different groups which use libraries, how and why libraries and library services are used, a quantitative
measure of user satisfaction, and user priorities for the future. The Task
Force has also laid the foundation for a more sustained and integrated
Libraries assessment program.

After six years, it's now time . . . to put into place a more comprehensive assessment program. We recommend the appointment of
an Assessment Librarian to develop an ongoing program and lead and
coordinate assessment efforts in the Libraries.

While the library assessment coordinator position was included in the libraries' list of new positions, budget reductions precluded filling it. Instead, a new
Library Assessment Group was formed with a broader charge to support "the
University Libraries programs and services through development and implementation of appropriate evaluation and assessment measures. The Group
will provide clear and timely reports and results. The Group will also work with
other assessment efforts on campus as well as provide support and expertise
for other assessment activities within the Libraries."

The specific responsibilities of the Library Assessment Group were to
coordinate the libraries' measurement, evaluation, and assessment activities;
develop and implement an ongoing assessment program in support of the
libraries programs, services, and operations; employ appropriate tools, techniques, and measures to acquire information needed for ongoing user needs
assessment; develop criteria to measure service quality; provide support and
expertise for other assessment efforts undertaken in the libraries; dissemi-
nate assessment information in a clear, timely, and appropriate manner to
library staff, the campus community, and the profession; and collaborate with
other campus units in related assessment and evaluation efforts.

The link between a user-centered focus and assessment was further developed with the concept of a "culture of assessment" in the UW Libraries that
would be a necessary corollary of the user-centered library. Local discussions
on this concept started in 1994 and Betsy Wilson, associate director of public services, developed it further, along with Amos Lakos of the University
of Waterloo and Shelley Phipps of the University of Arizona. This led to a
definition of a culture of assessment as "an environment in which decisions
are based on facts, research and analysis, and where services are planned and
delivered in ways that maximize positive outcomes and impacts for library
clients. A *culture of assessment* is an integral part of the process of change and

the creation of a user-centered library."[4] This concept also fit our own model of a coordinated but decentralized approach to library assessment.

Building Effective, Sustainable and Practical Library Assessment, 1999–2005

The 1999–2003 Strategic Plan identified "Assess and evaluate the effectiveness of our programs and services" as an overriding theme, noting that

> academic libraries everywhere are being required by their institutions to demonstrate the outcomes and efficacy of funded programs. The rapid pace of change and increasing expectations of users necessitate continuous examination of library programs and the internal practices and resources that support them.
>
> An ongoing assessment program not only provides valuable information with which we can plan for innovative and cost-effective new library services, but it also responds to our commitment to ensuring that public money is spent wisely and effectively.[5]

The continued growth of libraries assessment efforts made it difficult to rely on a volunteer committee for ongoing support and sustainability. The Library Assessment Group and others in the libraries continued to state the case for someone to have formal designation as library assessment coordinator. Steve Hiller, head of the Science Libraries and chair of the Library Assessment Group, was appointed as half-time library assessment coordinator in late 1999 (he continued as head of the Science Libraries). The Library Assessment Group charge was revised to reflect this change, and tasked to work with the library assessment coordinator to initiate and support library assessment efforts within the University Libraries; develop an ongoing, sustainable assessment program; identify user needs and assess the libraries' efforts at meeting them; foster a culture of assessment within the libraries; provide support as needed for assessment efforts conducted by other library staff; develop expertise and understanding of assessment measures and techniques and share these with library staff as needed; conduct the libraries' triennial user surveys; and communicate assessment activities and results to appropriate individuals and groups.

While information about the UW assessment program had been presented at conferences and survey information was available on the libraries' website, there was no published record other than articles in the libraries newsletter *Library Directions*. That changed in 2001 with the publication in *Library Trends* of an article based on a presentation at an Association of Research Libraries–sponsored symposium in October 2000 on measuring service quality.[6] Presentations made at national and international conferences from 2001 to 2005 were published in proceedings, papers, and journals and that practice has continued.

The UW Libraries was also recognized as an institutional, regional, and national leader in assessment. The Northwest Commission on Colleges and Universities in its 2003 decennial accreditation review of the University of Washington commended the libraries' commitment to effective assessment, stating that "planning, assessment and continuous improvement are ongoing processes with broad staff participation. The libraries' program for the measurement of library use and user satisfaction has resulted in ten years of longitudinal data and satisfaction rates and user behavior. This information is frequently referred to and used to modify existing services and plan new ones." The UW Libraries received the Association of College and Research Libraries' 2004 Excellence in Libraries award for research libraries. The award statement noted that "the UW Libraries have developed exemplary programs including innovative digital collections and services, information literacy for the UW campus, an assessment centered culture, and creative staff development and training."

In August 2004, Steve Hiller was appointed as a visiting program officer for assessment at the Association of Research Libraries (ARL). He joined Jim Self of the University of Virginia Library and Martha Kyrillidou at ARL in developing a service called "Making Library Assessment Work" (later renamed "Effective, Sustainable and Practical Library Assessment"). Both the University of Virginia Library and the UW Libraries were well-known leaders in the library assessment field. Recognizing that the usage and successful implementation of LibQUAL+ had provided copious amounts of assessment-related data, the goals of this service were to enable libraries to better utilize this information for change and improvement. A special focus was on the organizational structure that would facilitate and sustain success. The service consisted of a one and one-half day visit to a participating library followed by a report summarizing the participating library's current situation and recommendations for moving assessment forward. Forty-three libraries participated in this service between 2005 and 2010.

Integrating Planning and Assessment, 2006–2011

While the strategic plans for 2002–2005 and 2006–2010 reaffirmed the libraries' user-centered focus and the role of assessment in understanding user needs and evaluating program effectiveness, ongoing operational and management support for these plans was not well-defined.[7] A staff commit-tee worked with the Libraries Cabinet (administration) to craft the plans, but implementation and review were the responsibilities of the cabinet and man-agers. While a number of the objectives in each strategic plan included some form of measurement, these were rarely reviewed or assessed.

As the scope of assessment activities continued to expand and deepen, the libraries made the commitment to create an organizational place for assess-ment with a full-time director responsible for both assessment and planning. The alignment and better integration of assessment with planning were seen as strengthening overall organizational performance and accountability.

The Office of Assessment and Planning was established in early 2006 with Steve Hiller appointed as director. The director is responsible for providing leadership and vision for the libraries' assessment and planning activities, ensuring that assessment, measurement, planning, and analysis are integral parts of the libraries' programs and services. The director oversees assessment efforts within the University Libraries, serving as an internal consultant for assessment activities conducted by other library staff and working with the libraries' areas to analyze and report assessment data. The director represents the libraries in campus, regional, and national assessment efforts; evaluates the effectiveness of library assessment efforts; and recommends ways to strengthen the libraries' assessment and measurement program. He creates and maintains a sustainable planning environment and provides informa-tion, analysis, and reports to support the libraries' planning and management activities. Lastly, the director establishes, manages, and provides access to management information; and coordinates the ARL statistics and handles other centrally reported data and requests such as ARL SPEC kits and IPEDS surveys. The director reports to the senior associate dean who is responsible for library administrative services.

To provide additional support for assessment, a temporary half-time position titled management information librarian was created. This position works under the general direction of the director of assessment and planning and is responsible for supporting assessment efforts within the University Libraries. The management information librarian assists in the development, implementation, and management of a program to select and provide access to data and statistics collected by the libraries. This individual contributes to the compilation of a libraries data/fact site and print counterpart and main-tains and enhances the Libraries Assessment website.

The UW Libraries continues to be an active participant in the national and international assessment arenas. In 2006 the management information librarian and a colleague at the University of Virginia Libraries coauthored an ARL SPEC Kit on Library Assessment, to provide guidance for librarians developing assessment programs at their institutions.[8] The UW Libraries was one of three cofounders and organizers of the Library Assessment Conference which has been held every two years since 2006. In addition to helping organize the conferences, UW librarians have been active participants, presenting papers and posters on such topics as local surveys, e-metrics, usability, qualitative studies, the Balanced Scorecard, teaching and learning, and the culture of assessment. UW librarians have also presented at each of the Northumbria International Conferences on Performance Measurement in Libraries and Information Services since 2001.

In 2008 the Library Assessment Group was renamed the Libraries Assessment and Metrics Team (LAMT) and given a revised charge to assist in assessing organizational performance through the development of outcomes and success metrics; to help develop a management information infrastructure to make data and key statistics available to staff and the public; to maintain the Library Assessment website; and to plan the semiannual library assessment forums.

LAMT is now responsible for helping to plan the Triennial Survey and the In-Library Use Survey, and for reorganizing the presentation of assessment and library statistical information on the libraries' website. The assessment page is publicly available and provides information about the membership and charge of the Libraries Assessment and Metrics Team as well as presentations, publications, and reports produced by its members. The website promotes transparency in assessment efforts by providing links to results, survey forms, and summaries for the Triennial and In-Library Use surveys. In that same vein of transparency, the libraries' statistics are also publicly accessible through the website.

Midway through our 2006–2010 Strategic Plan, the Office of Assessment and Planning began to explore alternatives that could better support development and overall management of the planning process. Our five-year plans produced a number of successful initiatives, including the user-centered-library and the anytime-anyplace library that are cornerstones of our programs and services today—but over time the process for creating each new strategic plan took longer, was time- and labor-intensive, and was overly detailed and inclusive. The "strategic" focus was often overwhelmed by the number of goals and objectives and the links with weak oversight, execution, and measurement. Many of our staff began to see strategic planning as an exercise that was separate from and not tied to their ongoing work.

We began looking in 2008 at other organizational planning and performance models, seeking a program that was truly strategic, with focused priorities and choices, and that allowed us to spend less time on process and more on strategy and defining key outcomes that could be aligned with organizational capacity and resources. The model we desired would allow us to be sufficiently nimble and agile to adapt to environmental, economic, and institutional changes, as a five-year plan is too long. Such a model would need to integrate closely with our long-established assessment program where data had been used to inform programs and services but not necessarily linked to measuring progress on goals and objectives in the strategic plan. Further, the model we sought must involve staff in meaningful efforts to align workflows and responsibilities tied to strategic priorities and actions, and align with nascent university efforts to develop and implement a more rigorous planning process

In autumn 2008, the ARL began discussions on using the Balanced Scorecard as an organizational performance model in libraries. We were attracted by the focus on aligning strategy with metrics in a balanced framework that emphasized services to customers and stakeholders based on internal activities and a foundation of staff learning and expertise. The UW Libraries was one of four ARL libraries to participate in the "Library Scorecard" pilot that began in 2009.

The ARL pilot was an opportunity to test the applicability of the Scorecard to strategic planning in the libraries and learn from our consultants as well as our cohorts. We used the "priorities" that were identified in our 2006–2010 Strategic Plan for our test scorecard. They were placed in the Scorecard framework and we worked with key individuals to develop outcomes and measures. Our takeaways from the Scorecard pilot were to define outcomes before developing measures, balance existing data with new data collection, and the realization that strategy drives metrics.

We were sufficiently pleased with the Strategy Map and Scorecard that they became the framework for our new 2011–2013 Strategic Plan.[9] (See figure 1.2.) As we build out our thirteen key objectives, staff who work most closely in those areas develop actions, outcomes, time lines, and suggest possible metrics. Metrics are reviewed by both the Strategic Planning Action Team and the Libraries Assessment and Metrics Team. Our Strategy Map concisely shows who we are and where we want to be to both our staff and the campus community—Mission and Strategic Directions (which are represented in the Customer and Stakeholder areas) frame the perspectives/objectives with a firm underpinning of organizational values. Our Strategy Map and Scorecard also are aligned with university initiatives related to student and faculty success as well as cost efficiencies and effectiveness.

In 2009 the director of assessment and planning joined the Libraries Cabinet (administrative leadership group) and took responsibility for the next strategic plan and for preparing the narrative for the annual budget submission to the university. Budget submissions in 2010 and 2011 began using the Balanced Scorecard as a framework for organizational performance,

FIGURE 1.2

University Libraries, University of Wisconsin, 2011–2013 Strategy Map

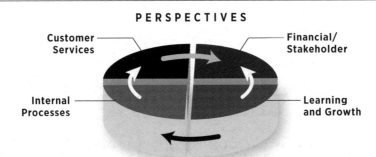

PERSPECTIVES

Customer Services — Financial/Stakeholder

Internal Processes — Learning and Growth

Customer Services
- Enhance UW teaching and learning
- Advance research and scholarship
- Provide productive and engaging library spaces

Internal Processes
- Apply and assess new subject librarian framework
- Realign online and print services support
- Review and revise collections and digitization strategies
- Create a sustainable foundation for delivering and assessing teaching and learning

Financial/Stakeholder
- Develop a sustainable academic business plan

Learning and Growth
- Align organizational capacity and structure with resources
- Focus staff expertise/work on strategic priorities/actions
- Provide infrastructures that support users and staff work

buttressed by local assessment data and comparative benchmarking statistics with peer ARL libraries.

Assessment Activities: Local Surveys

The University of Washington Libraries is well known for its program of large-scale cyclical user surveys that have been conducted since 1992 (Triennial Survey). More than just satisfaction surveys, these surveys have provided invaluable information about how students and faculty use the libraries, their library and information needs and priorities, and the importance and contributions of the libraries during a period of rapid change in the information and higher education environments. Additional local cyclical surveys include an In-Library Use Survey and a library staff Diversity and Organizational Climate

Survey. The Triennial and In-Library Use surveys have been adapted by a number of other libraries

Triennial Survey

For the first survey in 1992, the Task Force on Library Services worked with the UW Office of Educational Assessment (OEA) on the logistics and design of the survey. The task force arrived at several decisions concerning methodology that served as a foundation for future surveys:

- The survey would be run during the spring quarter.
- The survey population was defined as faculty, graduate and professional students, and undergraduates.
- Separate surveys would be designed for each group, although there would be a number of common questions.
- All faculty would be surveyed and a random sample of each student group taken.
- The survey would be mailed directly to the survey population.
- The survey would be returned to a nonlibrary campus unit for data entry.
- A small incentive would be offered for submission of surveys.

The OEA pulled the student samples from the registrar's database and the faculty names from the payroll database. Surveys were sent to 3,900 faculty and samples of 1,000 graduate and professional students and 1,000 undergraduates. The OEA also arranged for data entry and analysis, providing SPSS printouts of frequency responses (and means) for each group and cross-tabs by college/school and department for each group. The aggregate results for each group (including comments) were distributed to staff and academic program-specific information was distributed to subject librarians and unit heads. A short report on survey results was also included in the fall 1992 issue of *Library Directions*, a UW Libraries newsletter that was distributed to all UW faculty, library donors, regional and ARL libraries, and other interested parties. The 1992 results showed high satisfaction rates for all groups and that students, especially undergraduates, were the primary users of the physical library. Comments from undergraduates indicated that staff at some service desks did not take them seriously. Nearly 50 percent of faculty and graduate student respondents and 25 percent of undergraduates said they had connected remotely to the online catalog. While approximately 25 percent of faculty and graduate students had connected remotely to an online biblio-graphic database, only 2 percent of undergraduates had. Lastly, the top three priorities were the same for each group—build collections, improve the online catalog, and add bibliographic databases.

The task force made several recommendations for follow-up actions, including online catalog improvement; recognizing undergraduates as the primary users of our physical spaces; making it easier to connect to library resources and services remotely; and ensuring that staff treated students respectfully. The latter led to the development of a "good customer service" class that all staff were required to participate in.

The strong administrative support of Director Betty Bengtson and the new associate director for public services, Betsy Wilson, was instrumental in getting the process for the 1992 survey started and ensuring that the results were used. The Kenneth S. Allen Endowment Fund, a large unrestricted endow-ment for the University Libraries, was also used to support the external costs of this survey and others that followed.

The 1992 survey (with some changes) was run again in 1995 and results showed a continued shift to use of online discovery tools and resources. For faculty and graduate students an increasing percentage of this use was done remotely, and remote library visits now surpassed visits to the physical library. While the majority of remote use still took place from campus offices and labs, 25 percent of the faculty reported connecting to online services and resources at least weekly from home. Survey data entry was done by the Office of Educational Assessment, but all of the analysis was conducted by two task force members using SPSS. With the successful completion of this second large-scale user survey of faculty and students, the survey was now optimisti-cally called the Triennial Survey. The three-year cycle seemed a good fit for the iterative processes of survey design, implementation, analysis, recommenda-tions, and resulting service improvements and changes.

Preparation for the 1998 Triennial Survey included working closely with the faculty councils on educational technology and university libraries as well as campus computing and communications on questions dealing with the use and impact of information technology. The definition of "faculty" was stan-dardized and this definition was used in all succeeding surveys. Separate sur-vey "inserts" were sent to faculty and graduate students in the biosciences (including health sciences) and the fine arts. Results showed that the fre-quency of faculty and graduate student visits from outside the library contin-ued to increase, especially from off campus, and bioscientists were willing to sacrifice print for online access.

Succeeding surveys in 2001, 2004, 2007, and 2010 kept a set of core ques-tions, eliminated others, and added new ones, including some on library impact and scholarly communication. The survey went from print to web-based in

FIGURE 1.3

UW Libraries Triennial Survey, Number of Respondents
and Response Rate 1992-2010

Group	2010	2007	2004	2001	1998	1995	1992
Faculty	1,634 (39%)	1,455 (36%)	1,560 (40%)	1,345 (36%)	1,503 (40%)	1,359 (31%)	1,108 (28%)
Graduate/ Professional Students (UWS)	640 (32%)	580 (33%)	627 (40%)	597 (40%)	457 (46%)	409 (41%)	560 (56%)
Undergrads (UWS)	365 (16%)	467 (20%)	502 (25%)	497 (25%)	787 (39%)	463 (23%)	407 (41%)

FIGURE 1.4

Overall Satisfaction by Group: Triennial Survey, 1998-2010

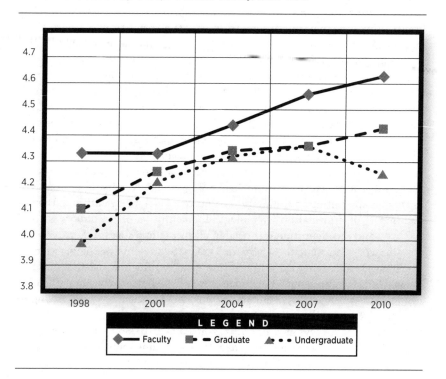

LEGEND
Faculty   Graduate   Undergraduate

2004. Related but separate surveys for UW Bothell and UW Tacoma students were done for the first time in 2007. Faculty from these schools were included in the survey population beginning with the 1998 surveys. The 2010 survey was run at a time of severe budget retrenchment at the university. The number of faculty respondents (1,634), and library importance, impact, and satisfaction were the highest ever recorded. However, undergraduate satisfaction dropped, related to overcrowding of library facilities. (See figures 1.3 and 1.4.)

In-Library Use Survey

The UW Libraries first developed and implemented an In-Library Use Survey in 1993 to acquire information about nonaffiliated visitors and their use of library services. An elaborate sampling procedure was established that consisted of random two-hour survey periods at the then twenty campus libraries. Those exiting the library during these periods were asked their status and, if not university-affiliated, were given a short survey to complete. This method provided data on the percent of nonaffiliated users exiting the library as well as their activities in the library. Similar surveys were conducted in 1996 and 1999 but were limited to the five largest campus libraries due to the relatively small numbers of nonaffiliated users in most branch libraries and the consequent large number of sampling sessions needed. There were some changes in questions between the surveys to capture new information, especially related to technology and the use of online resources. Significant changes in in-library use patterns were observed among both nonaffiliated users and the University of Washington community during the 1990s. The 1999 exit survey revealed a continuing decline in the proportion of nonaffiliated users in the largest libraries to approximately 10 percent of all users.

Information about University of Washington student and faculty use of library facilities came from transactional data and also through the Triennial Survey. However, with the continued decrease in the frequency of faculty and graduate student visits to the physical library, surveying users in library facilities was seen as a more precise method for acquiring information about who was using our libraries, why they visited, and what they did during their visits, regardless of affiliation. In 2002 the In-Library Use Survey was given to everyone entering the library during designated survey periods. Survey methodology and distribution remained reasonably consistent in subsequent surveys run in 2005, 2008, and 2011. One-page surveys were distributed to those entering the library during two-hour time periods in May and completed surveys were returned as users exited the library. Approximately 4,000 surveys were returned during each survey year, and they confirmed the importance of the library as place for undergraduate students. The surveys over those years

FIGURE 1.5

In-Library Use Survey, Number of Respondents by Group 2001–2011:
Sessions in Common at UW Seattle

	2011	2008	2005	2002
Undergraduates	2,495 (74%)	2,210 (69%)	2,091 (64%)	2,304 (59%)
Graduate/ Professional Students	588 (17%)	640 (20%)	723 (22%)	986 (25%)
Faculty/Staff	130 (4%)	166 (5%)	168 (5%)	251 (7%)
Nonaffiliated	128 (4%)	154 (5%)	250 (8%)	312 (8%)
Did not state	38 (1%)	26 (1%)	34 (1%)	25 (1%)

FIGURE 1.6

What Respondents Did in the Library by Group: 2011 In-Library Use Survey

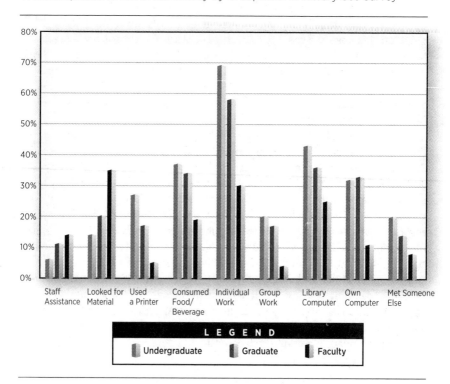

FIGURE 1.7

Activities during Library Visit: 2011/2012 In-Library Use Survey

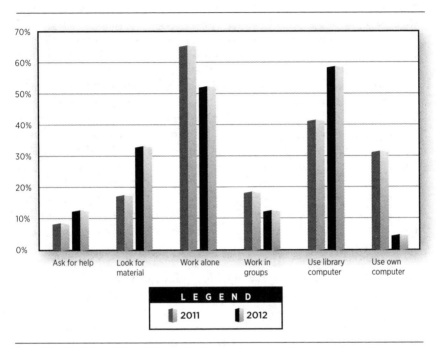

showed a steady increase in the percentage of respondents who were undergraduates—reaching 75 percent in 2011. Survey results that year also showed a decline in the use of library computers and a substantial increase in the use of personal computing devices. (See figures 1.5, 1.6, and 1.7.)

Diversity and Organizational Climate Survey

In 2004 the libraries designed and conducted its first Diversity and Organizational Climate Survey. Survey results showed that communication needed improvement, and a number of steps were taken to facilitate communication at all levels. Similar surveys were run in 2008 and 2011 and showed improvement in communication and diversity importance and action. However, three years of budget reductions with no salary increases were factors in low ratings for staff support and recognition.

Other Assessment Activities

While the Triennial Survey remains the centerpiece of the assessment program, it is part of a suite of assessment activities that began to coalesce in the 1995–99 period. This suite includes e-metrics, usability, other qualitative assessment methods, and collaborative assessment both within and external to the university.

The work on e-metrics is led by Tim Jewell and colleagues in the Libraries Information Resources and Scholarly Communication program. Jewell served as an ARL visiting program officer in 1995–96 with a focus on expenditures for electronic resources.[10] His ARL work led to the development of several questions on the ARL Supplementary Statistics Survey that deal with electronic resource usage and costs. Jewell has continued working with e-metrics and had significant involvement in the development of Electronic Resources Management systems (ERM), including Project SUSHI during the past ten years and in several NISO working groups. More recent e-metrics work has involved developing different methods of determining the value of e-journals and e-journal packages.

The UW Libraries' first website was established in autumn 1994 and its content was tweaked on an annual basis through 1997 by libraries staff, although with little input from the user community. In 1998 a major redesign of the website was undertaken with the goal of refocusing it from a library-centric organizational structure to that of an "information gateway" which would enable users to find information that they needed without knowing how the library was organized. The libraries collaborated with the UW Department of Technical Communications in conducting usability testing with students developing the usability protocols and processes. Testing was done in the department's usability lab, which contained a number of tools to support different evaluation methods. Significant changes were made to the navigation and terminology used on the new site as a result of usability testing. Usability testing became an integral part of web design, and the libraries acquired equipment and expertise to perform its own usability testing beginning in 2001. Subsequent usability efforts have taken place under the aegis of the libraries' Information Technology Services, and notable activities have included WorldCat local implementation, LibGuides, and digital library initiatives.[11] The libraries has also used wayfinding to examine the "usability" of library physical space.

Qualitative information about library services and resources has traditionally been derived primarily from survey and suggestion box comments, faculty councils, reference transactions, and interactions between subject libraries and faculty and graduate students. While survey comments are analyzed and categorized, most other qualitative input was not subject to a systematic analysis. In 1998 the libraries conducted its first set of structured focus groups, focusing on the biosciences and the fine arts. The bioscience focus groups (faculty and graduate students) centered on the use of resources, especially electronic resources, while the fine arts focus groups dealt primarily with the concept of a central fine arts library that would consolidate existing libraries for art, drama, and music. Information gleaned from these focus groups was used both in planning and for the libraries' 1998 Triennial Survey, which featured special inset surveys for faculty and students in those areas.

Focus groups have been conducted in such areas as interlibrary loan, teaching and learning, research needs, scholarly communication, disabled student services, and use of electronic and print resources. Three library advisory groups (faculty, graduate and professional students, and undergraduates) also provide structured input on topics ranging from discovery tools to collaborative work spaces.

Observational studies have also proven valuable, especially for time-sensitive information. Observational studies on the use of services and the use of facilities and equipment at specific times of the day have helped adjust the location of library computers and desk staffing. Guided observation and interviews have been completed, focusing on faculty and graduate student searching methods in bibliographic databases and how faculty find and use electronic journals. These studies proved quite useful in the development of search interfaces.

User surveys in the 1990s revealed that students, especially undergraduates, were the primary users of library facilities. Planning for new and renovated space prior to that time had focused mainly on faculty and library staff needs. As use of library space shifted from a collections focus to a user focus, efforts were made to gain input from users about their space needs. For example, users had the opportunity to try out furniture for renovations in the Odegaard Undergraduate and Suzzallo-Allen libraries during internal renovations. In general, however, such input was collected indirectly and not in any systematic or structured manner.

Two recent renovation projects, the Research Commons and the Odegaard Undergraduate Library, have adopted a user-centered design approach. While the Odegaard renovation planning process has just started, students are already involved in focus groups, and design concepts. The architectural firm responsible for the renovation of the Research Commons space employed a user-centered design process that involved charettes and other user involvement throughout the design process, including furniture and equipment evaluation.

To create a collaborative environment in which students and faculty can come together to share and discuss research, as well as get support for all steps of the research process, the design of the Research Commons involved the reconfiguration of 15,500 square feet in the Allen Library into a new type of space. When the doors opened in October 2010 it was clear that this space was different than any other in the libraries. The majority of the furniture was movable for unlimited seating configurations; there were whiteboard surfaces on the walls and tables; and new collaborative technology areas with plasma screens were available for sharing laptop images.

The same user-centered approach to design that had proven so successful was also used to assess how the space was being used. Research Commons staff employed several techniques to evaluate why users came to the space, what users did in the space, and whether the space fostered collaboration. Evaluation methods included observation, discussion groups, and a short survey in spring 2011. Both the discussion groups and the short survey specifically asked visitors how they used the space. Each assessment method verified the findings of the others: users identified the Commons as collaborative work space and enjoyed the ability to customize their work environment with the flexible furniture and equipment available to them.

The findings from the survey were even more powerful when compared with results from the In-Library Use Survey for nonusers of the Research Commons. By comparing those two surveys we discovered that those who used the Research Commons tended to use the library for longer periods of time and used more of the services and resources offered by the libraries. Changes made based on the results of the discussion groups and surveys included removal of some computer workstations and rearrangement of others to deemphasize their use as individual work space, and two new reservable group areas were created to allow for more and larger group activities.

Collaborative Assessment

The UW Libraries have worked on collaborative assessment efforts with campus, organizational, and other institutional partners. The collaborative approach provides additional expertise and perspectives that enable richer assessments.

Collaborative assessment efforts with campus partners started in 1994 around the use of information technology in teaching and learning, especially in the UWired program. UWired began in autumn 1994 as a collaborative effort among four university units (including the libraries) to help integrate information technology and electronic information resources into the curriculum. A UWired evaluation group was established to develop a formative assessment program based on evaluation of the various program components to support the development and ongoing improvement of UWired offerings. Assessment actions included surveying new students and measuring use of the Center for Teaching and Learning Technology. Course evaluations focused on competencies and outcomes and establishing outcomes for the major UWired activities outside of courses.

The libraries expanded collaboration with the Office of Educational Assessment and helped add questions relating to library use and satisfaction to the OEA's annual Senior Survey. Collaboration also extended outside the UW environment. The University of Washington was one of nine institutions that participated in the Coalition for Networked Information (CNI) project "Assessing the Academic Networked Environment" in 1997–98. The libraries was the lead party in the UW effort that focused on three major areas: use of networked information resources; teaching and learning; and library/information needs assessment. These areas built upon the libraries' established strengths in e-metrics, UWired, and user needs assessment. Project briefings on the UW experience in "Assessing the Academic Networked Environment" were given at the spring 1998 CNI conference and at the CAUSE conference in December 1998. A full-day pre-conference workshop on "Assessing the Academic Networked Environment" was given at the ACRL 9th National Conference in 1999, with three of the four presenters from the University of Washington.

The University Libraries was one of twelve participants in the ARL ServQUAL (later LibQUAL) pilot in 2000. The libraries participated in the pilot each year between 2000 and 2003 while still conducting its own surveys. When LibQUAL was finalized for 2004, the decision was made not to participate in that survey but to continue with our own. While the LibQUAL survey provided some useful information and offered the opportunity to compare results with other research libraries, we believed that local surveys could best capture information on user needs and priorities and respond to specific issues pertinent to the University of Washington. We also valued the survey data we had collected since 1992 and the ability to track changes and trends going forward.

The libraries continued to expand its assessment repertoire with new collaborative initiatives in information literacy and user-centered design. The UW Bothell Library has a long tradition of involvement with course and curricular design since its founding in 1991, helping to integrate information literacy concepts into the formal academic program. In 2006 Bothell librarians worked with English 102: Writing from Research faculty at the co-located community college to rate student work using rubrics. This has evolved into a more "practical and sustainable" method of student self-assessment integrated into the course. Identified positive outcomes from this assessment method include enhanced student learning, increased faculty-librarian collaboration, and higher visibility and relevance of the information literacy instruction program.[12] The effectiveness of this method has also been acknowledged through its inclusion in the Outcome Guide used for the course campuswide.

Further, the UW Bothell Library was one of five institutions selected to participate in the nationwide Rubric Assessment of Information Literacy Skills (RAILS) project that began in 2010. Samples of student work were collected and evaluated not only with the purpose of assessing students' learning, but also to gauge how well the librarians and faculty were assessing that learning.

Conclusion

The past twenty years have seen library assessment at the University of Washington grow from an initial survey to a multifaceted assessment program that is centered on customer-centered organizational performance within an integrated planning and assessment framework. The libraries is recognized at the University of Washington as an institutional leader in assessment and performance measurement. This has played a key role in decisions to increase investment in the libraries. As the university moves to a data-driven allocation model, it is critical that the libraries present supportive and compelling data that demonstrates its value to the university community.

NOTES

1. University of Washington Libraries, "UW Libraries Assessment," http://lib .washington.edu/assessment/.
2. University of Washington Libraries, "University of Washington Libraries Mission and Strategic Plan," 1991, www.lib.washington.edu/about/ strategicplan/archive/1991/view.
3. University of Washington Libraries, "University of Washington Libraries Strategic Plan 1995–1999," 1995, www.lib.washington.edu/about/ strategicplan/archive/1995/view.
4. Amos Lakos, Betsy Wilson, and Catherine Larson, "Building a Culture of Assessment in Academic Libraries" (paper presented at "Living the Future II" conference, Tucson, Arizona, April 21–24, 1998).
5. University of Washington Libraries, "Strategic Plan 1999–2003," 1999, www .lib.washington.edu/about/strategicplan/archive/1999/view.
6. Steve Hiller, "Assessing User Needs, Satisfaction, and Library Performance at the University of Washington Libraries," Library Trends 49 (2001): 605–25.
7. University of Washington Libraries, "Strategic Plan 2002–2005," 2002, www .lib.washington.edu/about/strategicplan/archive/2002-2005-strategic-plan/ view; University of Washington Libraries, "Vision 2010: The Libraries' 2006– 2010 Strategic Plan," 2010, www.lib.washington.edu/about/strategicplan/ archive/2006-2010-strategic-plan-vision-2010.

8. Stephanie P. Wright and Lynda S. White, *SPEC Kit 303: Library Assessment* (Washington, DC: Association of Research Libraries, 2007).

9. University of Washington Libraries, "Building Sustainable Futures: The UW Libraries 2011–2013 Strategic Plan," 2011, www.lib.washington.edu/about/strategicplan.

10. Julia C. Blixrud and Timothy D. Jewell, "Understanding Electronic Resources and Library Materials Expenditures: An Incomplete Picture," *ARL: A Bimonthly Report* 197 (1998).

11. Christine Tawatao et al., "LibGuides Usability Testing: Customizing a Product to Work for Your Users" (paper presented at the Library Assessment Conference, Baltimore, Maryland, October 24–27, 2010).

12. Leslie Bussert, Karen Diller, and Sue F. Phelps, "Voices of Authentic Assessment: Stakeholder Experiences Implementing Sustainable Information Literacy Assessments" (paper presented at the Library Assessment Conference, Seattle, Washington, August 4–7, 2008).

LYNDA S. WHITE
University of Virginia Library

2
Tracking Our Performance

Assessment at the University of Virginia Library

THE UNIVERSITY OF VIRGINIA (U.VA) LIBRARY HAS BEEN IN-volved in assessment activities since at least 1921/22.1 The library was a contributor to James Thayer Gerould's statistical compilations and was a charter member of the ARL, joining in 1932. In the 1980s, simple data collection expanded to data analysis and involvement in persuading others of the value of using data to make decisions. The 1990s brought the addition of user surveys and the incorporation of user feedback into decision making, leading, at the end of the decade, to the creation of a Management Information Services (MIS) Department. This department has fostered assessment both at the library and elsewhere, through active involvement in the larger assessment community.

Founded in 1819, the University of Virginia is a nationally ranked institution of higher education. Located in Charlottesville, Virginia, it is renowned primarily for the humanities and its law, medical, and business professional schools, although recently there has been a push to strengthen the sciences. There are 14,700 undergraduate and 6,000 graduate and professional students; full-time instructional faculty number 1,200. The university offers bachelor's degrees in forty-seven fields, master's degrees in sixty-seven fields, six educational specialist degrees, two first-professional degrees (law and medicine), and doctoral degrees in fifty-five fields.

There are thirteen library facilities in the University of Virginia Library system, excluding the Law, Health Sciences, and Graduate Business professional school libraries which are not administratively part of the university library system. The thirteen U.Va libraries together hold 4.5 million volumes and provide access to 124,000 print and electronic journal titles. For the fiscal year 2011, the system circulated about 350,000 books and reserves, answered around 53,000 reference questions, and managed 56,000 items through interlibrary loan. There were 266 full-time equivalent staff and student workers and expenditures were $27,800,000.

The library's mission is to enable research, teaching, and learning through services, collections, tools, and spaces for the faculty and students of today and tomorrow. The library staff prides itself on customer service, innovation and risk taking, and learning and staff development. For example, we have been engaged in major digitization projects since 1992, and were among the first to install a coffee shop inside the library in 1998. There is a culture of change where our staff expects that things will not remain the same. Moreover, we have been collecting and using data about the library for many years. One of our guiding principles is that we "use data to make choices."

U.Va was fortunate to have Kendon Stubbs on staff for forty-two years, from where he retired as deputy university librarian in 2003.[2] Stubbs was an early proponent of collecting library statistics and of using data to make decisions. He published a widely cited article on library statistics in *College & Research Libraries* in 1981.[3] Stubbs not only contributed tremendously to the compilation of longitudinal data from the ARL statistics (he has been called the father of the ARL Index, which was instituted in 1980), he also had a profound impact on statistics gathering and other kinds of assessment at Virginia.[4] His constant focus was on our users and the performance of the library for their benefit. As Jim Self stated while presenting the Library Assessment Career Achievement Award to Stubbs at the 2010 Library Assessment Conference in Baltimore, "Kendon never forgot the reason for collecting data. They were not numbers for the sake of numbers. The data were collected so they could measure our performance, improve our service, and increase customer satisfaction."[5] Those qualities were only the beginning.

> Kendon's work goes well beyond statistics and assessment. . . . At his home library Kendon was a relentless innovator. He was creative in thinking up wild and crazy ideas, and practical enough to make them happen. . . . Under Kendon's leadership, the UVa Library became a data pioneer, conducting its first faculty survey in 1993, followed by a student survey the next year. The Management Information Services unit

was established in 1997. Four years later UVa became the first research
library in North America to implement the Balanced Scorecard.[6]

Kendon Stubbs was awarded the university's highest honor in 1998/99: the
Thomas Jefferson Award. This award recognizes excellence in service to the
university community and honors a faculty member who has "exemplified in
character, work, and influence the principles and ideals of Thomas Jefferson,
and thus [has] advanced the objectives for which Jefferson founded the University."[7] His shadow continues to influence assessment at the U.Va Library.

During the 1980s, the focus of assessment at Virginia was on data gathering. While we had contributed to the ARL annual survey for decades, various departments within the library also provided more in-depth data related
to their units. Size of collections data from the Cataloging Department, for
example, dated to at least 1971. Amassing this data became easier once our
integrated library system went live in 1989. In addition, deeper analysis of
circulation data began in earnest after we automated circulation processes
in 1982. Formal consolidated circulation reports were first issued by the
Resources Distribution Group in 1988/89.

Development of the User Survey Program

The U.Va Library began conducting user satisfaction surveys in the 1990s
under the aegis of the Management Information Committee. This committee was formed by Kendon Stubbs in 1990, with Jim Self as chair. Part of its
task was to educate staff about management information via presentations
at library-wide staff meetings. While the committee took over compilation
of circulation statistics in 1992/93, it also managed our first user surveys,
launching a faculty survey in 1993. This initial foray garnered a huge 70 percent response rate. The survey asked faculty for their opinions of our collections, services, and facilities with rating, ranking, multiple choice, and
open-ended questions.[8] The committee identified where library performance
could be enhanced using this management data. A survey of students followed
in 1994. These surveys laid the groundwork for twenty years of assessment
of our users' satisfaction with the library. The data collected from our survey program is used to make programmatic changes that enhance our users'
experiences of our services. As a result of the first surveys, for example, hours
were extended during intersessions and holidays, the Science and Engineering
Library was air-conditioned, and a more subject-oriented approach to collection development was instituted.

Since 2008 we have surveyed about a third of our user population every
year. We typically begin revising our questionnaire in late fall and field it
shortly after the spring semester starts. Our response rates have ranged

between 30 percent and 70 percent over the nearly two decades since our survey program began. By regularly querying our users, we have been able to collect a vast amount of data over time. Close analysis of the comment data has made it possible to spot trends in user needs.[9]

In addition to the surveys, in the mid-1990s, a two-year study of the circulation patterns of newly acquired monographs was conducted.[10] This study looked at books cataloged and made available to patrons in 1993, and then followed their circulation data for the next two years. Results indicated that English-language books had a 71 percent probability of circulating in the first two years of availability. Foreign-language books had a less than 33 percent chance of being used within this period. Use rates for both categories declined in the second year. This study, coupled with results from the first faculty survey, led to a radical change in our collection development policies and a complete reorganization of collection development functions within the library.[11] Copies of high-use materials were added to the collection; the Collection Development Department was disbanded, and a subject liaison program was created in its stead; and foreign-language acquisitions were reduced. This study was also the basis for one of our later Balanced Scorecard metrics and justified a change in collection development strategy from collecting for future scholars to collecting for current users.

The Evolution of the Management Information Services Department

In 1997 Jim Self, then director of Clemons Library, and Dave Griles, a library programmer, began to devote half of their time to the collection and compilation of data. Lynda White, from the Fine Arts Library, was invited to join them quarter time. In 2000, with Kendon Stubbs's blessing, the three became full-time members of the Management Information Services Department, working on assessment and data collection, analysis, and reporting.

Jim Self is the initial and current department director. He provides data for the library administration on demand, tallies survey data, researches assessment tools, and proselytizes about assessment in the greater library and beyond. Lynda White, the associate director, analyzes data and writes reports, coordinates departmental activities, collects and analyzes qualitative data, and collects data from various staff for reports and outside surveys. As a programmer and problem-solver, Dave Griles was responsible for putting our surveys on the Web starting in 1998, and for extracting the data, until we began using the online service Question Pro in 2010. He currently does programming for special studies to answer questions posed by various administrators and managers. For the first decade we also had a fifteen-hour-per-week intern to help with data analysis and reports.

FIGURE 2.1

Mission of the Management Information Services Department

Management Information Services (MIS) is responsible for coordinating and facilitating assessment activities for the University of Virginia Library. We collect and compile Library data for local and national agencies and for planning and decision making within the Library.

To accomplish these ends, MIS:

1. Cultivates a culture of assessment within the Library

2. Provides data, and analysis of data, about the University of Virginia Library

3. Provides usage statistics for electronic, physical, and other resources

4. Reviews, and assists with, applications to the University of Virginia Institutional Review Board for Social and Behavioral Sciences (IRB) for projects involving human subjects

5. Reviews and assists with developing surveys of our user and staff populations

6. Evaluates assessment projects and works with staff to determine the appropriate assessment tools for each situation

7. Develops expertise in various techniques of data collection and analysis, including focus groups and customer surveys, as well as analysis of quantitative and qualitative data

8. Educates Library staff as to the value of collecting and using management information

9. Provides assistance in implementing assessment projects

10. Works with other groups in the Library that perform assessment.

Source: University of Virginia Library, Management Information Services, www2.lib.virginia.edu/mis/index.html.

In 2009 we acquired a four-hour-per-week staff share position to deal with collecting electronic resource usage data. This is an extremely complicated and time-consuming process that MIS has been managing since 2000. We tried to rely on graduate students to do this for nearly a decade, but this solution was not entirely satisfactory. Dedicating a staff person to managing the collection of this data means that we no longer have to constantly train new students in the mysteries of serials, COUNTER, and access to data from numerous vendors with a variety of reporting mechanisms. While we did flirt with outsourcing some of this work to a vendor, that process proved insufficient to justify the cost. This task will soon be turned over to a new electronic resources librarian position.

MIS has constantly adjusted what data we collect, how we collect that data, and how we manage projects in order to streamline procedures and take advantage of differing or newly acquired staff skills. We also continued the practice started by the Management Information Committee of informing our library colleagues about the uses of data through presentations at town meetings, classes on statistics, and visits to departments.

Our current mission (figure 2.1) has not changed appreciably from our initial one, although a few items were added as our assessment repertoire grew. In general, we coordinate assessment activities for the library by collecting, compiling, and analyzing data for the library, university, and national agencies, whether it is numerical data about our operations or qualitative data from our users.

Selected MIS Projects

One of the earliest projects undertaken by MIS was a SERVQUAL survey done in 1998.[12] Based partially on a similar study by the Texas A&M University Library, the effort colored our willingness to participate in early LibQUAL surveys.[13] We discovered that users were very annoyed with the instrument itself. Specifically, they were reluctant to answer the same question twice, even when the response options were listed side by side. Nonetheless, we gained very valuable information from the survey. It sparked the idea of providing customer service training for our desk student workers by pointing out that often only student staff were available after 5:00 p.m. and that their responsiveness and accuracy were less than adequate.

While SERVQUAL was an interesting local assessment, by 2006 we wanted to compare our library to others across North America, so we participated in ARL's LibQUAL survey that fall. This survey yielded some interesting results. Our journal holdings, in particular, were an issue of dissatisfaction for faculty, leading MIS to conduct ten-minute follow-up interviews with eighty-two faculty members in departments across the university. Factors fueling faculty dissatisfaction ranged from a need for more foreign journals and back files to many issues with searching and accessing both print and electronic journals. The MIS director then further analyzed faculty data by discipline, and compared results with the thirty-seven ARL libraries that participated in the 2006 LibQUAL survey.[14] This comparison illustrated the importance of journals to faculty at ARL institutions, and that faculty expressed dissatisfaction with the participating libraries' collections regardless of their collection's size. This study was replicated in 2009 by Columbia University Libraries with similar results.[15]

In 1999/2000, MIS staff inaugurated a benchmarking project to assess the library's shelving process.[16] Using the University of Arizona and Virginia Tech libraries as benchmarking partners, we gathered data about our own process, and compared it to our partners' processes. We streamlined the shelving process, and instituted constant quality checks and data collection as part of the process. With actual data available on the improvements resulting from the new process and prodigious goals, including shelving all returned books within four hours and shelf reading three books on each side of the newly shelved book, we were able to convince our library administration to provide additional funding. These goals later became a Balanced Scorecard metric. MIS participated in one further benchmarking project, on staff training, which honed our skills and allowed us to add the process to our repertoire of services offered.

In 2000 we also produced our first consolidated annual library statistical report, combining reports from various departments and units about a variety of library functions with a summary of the data submitted for the ARL annual survey. This was and continues to be a major undertaking, as the reports contain extensive analyses of circulation and size of collections data, along with examination of long-term trends; usage data for electronic journals, reference sources, e-books and LibGuides; reference and instruction data; budget and fund-raising data; collections expenditures; interlibrary loan and document delivery statistics; and data related to preservation, staff training, shelving, gate counts, and facilities. With changes in presentation and the kinds of data reported, the report continues to be produced and used by staff eleven years later. It has also been posted to our website since 2002, so that the data are available to all staff and to others interested in library assessment.[17] We now have a considerable amount of longitudinal data that helps us identify trends and needs in our library.

In early 2000, MIS noticed from the reference statistics we collected for ARL that the use of reference services was declining. Determined to find out why, in 2001 we hired an outside facilitator to query groups of faculty, graduate students, and undergraduate students about their use of our reference services. We were surprised by the results. While our users were beginning to use Google to answer queries, they also indicated that they were using our website to answer their basic questions. They liked to find information for themselves without mediation from staff, and we had made it easy for them to do that on our website and by providing online resources and databases with full text. We also learned a great deal by observing our outside facilitator and, after some additional reading and study, we added focus groups to our growing repertoire of assessment tools.

The Balanced Scorecard Project

One of MIS's biggest undertakings was to institute a Balanced Scorecard at the UV Library. The Balanced Scorecard is a management tool that we adapted to reflect our library's vision and culture and to provide a comprehensive snapshot of our library's overall health.[18] Our library was interested in implementing the Scorecard to gain control of the large amount of data we collected. Furthermore, we wanted a better overall view of our performance, to see whether we were successful in meeting our goals. The Scorecard forced us to determine what our most important day-to-day operations were, in terms of the ones we wanted to measure, as well as where we wanted to go with new programs.

The Scorecard balances four perspectives: the *customer*, or our users' needs or customer service; *internal processes*, or how well we manage our processes to provide customer service; *finance*, or what it costs us to provide our materials and services; and *learning and growth*, or how well we are positioned to learn and change as our users' needs change. While we did not develop an enterprise-level strategy map at the time we first implemented the Scorecard, we did devise two to four strategies for each perspective. These strategies defined what we believed our library is about, or what was most important to us. Each strategy had one to three metrics to measure how well we were doing, and each metric had two targets or goals, with the first target requiring complete success and the second, partial success. Failure, of course, was an option. This allowed the Balanced Scorecard to serve as a red flag, identifying areas where we needed to make improvements or find additional resources to accomplish goals.

Work on developing our Scorecard began in April 2001. A steering committee was formed along with four subcommittees, one for each Balanced Scorecard perspective. One advantage to this method was that over thirty staff members were involved, again nurturing our culture of assessment. As none of us had any experience with this tool, there was a considerable learning curve in developing our Scorecard. Metrics were finalized by September 2001. We used July 1, 2001, as our starting date for gathering data for our first Scorecard, for 2002.

We initially chose twenty-six metrics, although this proved very difficult to limit. Equally important, we had to minimize the costs of collecting the data in terms of both labor and dollars. We used existing measurements wherever possible. We also tried to use data that could be efficiently mined from existing databases. Rather than counting every action, we used sampling for some metrics. This included, for example, measuring how many items acquired were actually used or what percentage of our equipment was working effectively at any given moment. We were very careful not to unduly overburden staff with data collection tasks and to make sure that what we measured was indicative of our performance.

Some of the types of metrics we developed included customer service ratings from our user survey; timeliness of service measures, such as speed of our delivery service, or reshelving materials; cost of service measures, including what it costs to order a new book or acquire an item on interlibrary loan;

number of uses by patrons of the library's recall service, electronic journals, or special collections materials; success in acquiring funding, including the percentage of fund-raising dollars that are unrestricted; and comparisons with peers, using tools such as the ARL rankings. While our focus was on our users, we also measured things that affected staff, such as job satisfaction, the value of our staff training program, comparison of staff salaries to peer groups, and ethnic diversity.

We determined at the outset that our metrics and targets would be reviewed each year to see whether they were still valuable and whether there were any "outliers" that needed adjustment. We revised our Scorecard each year through 2010, growing it to forty-one measures before reducing it to "Balanced Scorecard Lite" with only four metrics in 2010. At this time, the library undertook an extensive revision and re-visioning of its Scorecard, beginning with creating the library-wide strategy map that was lacking in the first Scorecard. New metrics will be in place by 2013.

The Balanced Scorecard has been productive for us. One metric, for example, dealt with how quickly we acquired and made available books requested by patrons for purchase. We had long thought we were doing this in seven days. Once we figured out a way to measure our process, we discovered that we were meeting this goal only 17 percent of the time. A group was quickly formed to find ways to improve the process.

Another initiative that also became a Balanced Scorecard metric involved testing the usability of our library's websites. Although we had recently revised all of our websites, there were still concerns about ease of use by our users. In 2004 the MIS director proposed that the library hire an intern to do systematic heuristic and usability testing. A library-wide Web Usability Committee was formed with the MIS director as chair. While there was a learning curve similar to that for the Balanced Scorecard for members of the MIS staff and the Web Usability Committee, the experience expanded our culture of assessment to more staff members.

Although the targets for the usability metric were not met the first year, a testing process was established, and the concept of testing websites by users who are not library staff gained credence. The metric became the responsibility of the Communication and Publications Department, which managed the website. In early 2007, an intensely engaged group of staff formed a User Requirements/Usability Community both to assist with website testing and to gather data on our users' ease of access to the collections and services we offered in our online library environment. An MIS staff member was initially part of this group. In 2010, one of the usability community founders formed the User Experience Team, which included an MIS member. This team had three specific goals: to manage the development of the user interface for our new discovery tool for the online catalog; to develop and test a new mobile devices website; and to develop and test a new portal to the research pages of the library's website.

MIS contributed data mined from various user surveys, and personas for one undergraduate and one graduate student, and for two faculty representing science and the humanities. The goals for this team were accomplished, and in 2011 our music librarian was reassigned half-time to a new permanent User Experience Team. This team now does extensive web usability testing, analysis, and revision.

As our Balanced Scorecard has evolved, we have added metrics about different aspects of the library's operations. Our initial Scorecard required a survey of staff to measure how well we treated *each other* as customers. This survey was a simple one-to-five rating of each department. The results revealed enough red flags that MIS followed up with structured interviews of nineteen staff members. We wanted to learn why there was dissatisfaction with service received from business services, administration, and library human resources. It was here that we first documented our organizational communication issues and uncovered other issues related to our work climate.

As the Balanced Scorecard steering committee discussed revisions for the metrics, we often talked about these work climate issues. We decided to add metrics for communication, job satisfaction, and training effectiveness to our Scorecard, but we questioned how to measure this. By 2003, the steering committee decided to use a survey of library staff to explore issues in these areas.

In 2003 we hired an associate university librarian (AUL) for organizational development who graciously shared a worklife questionnaire she had used at her previous institution.[19] We revised this survey to reflect the culture at U.Va. The instrument was grouped into seven sections: job satisfaction, interpersonal relations, communication and collaboration, diversity, resource availability, staff development, and health and safety. Each section contained positively worded statements about the topic and a box for open-ended comments. Respondents were asked to rate the statements on a scale of one to five, from strongly disagree to strongly agree. The MIS programmer transferred the survey to a web format so that the resulting data could be easily extracted and anonymity could be maintained. We fielded the survey for two weeks in June 2004.

Sixty-six percent of our 220 staff members participated. Our target was 80 percent agree or agree strongly, which we tabulated using the percentage of respondents who marked a statement either agree or agree strongly. We met the target on only one of the metrics. The question was how to improve those scores. Specific statements that were rated agree or agree strongly by fewer than 40 percent of staff gave us a good indication of where we needed to focus attention. The overall results for the sections on job satisfaction, communication, and staff development were used for the Balanced Scorecard metrics.

There was plenty of data from the survey for us to figure out broad areas that needed attention, but little detail on exactly what was the problem.

We decided to do focus groups with staff to get a handle on what exactly it was that staff were dissatisfied with. MIS facilitated these focus group discussions in the fall of 2004. Using volunteers, we set up four groups with approximately ten staff in each group. Nineteen percent of library staff participated. None of the participants' names were revealed to anyone but the MIS facilitator and the scheduler. We wanted staff to be open and honest, and to feel safe in expressing their views.

We were curious as to why 77 percent of staff enjoyed coming to work but only 59 percent were satisfied with their jobs, so we began each session by having participants talk about one thing they liked about working in the library. It was obvious from the discussion that these staff really did enjoy working at U.Va and with each other; the academic environment was key. We then talked about the low-scoring areas in each of the seven sections of the survey. Participants had quite a few good, doable ideas for making improvements. MIS, with assistance from an intern, compiled a list of issues and suggested solutions, and the AUL for organizational development took these, along with an action plan, to our senior administrative team. A number of changes were made based on the feedback we had received. Most of the changes were relatively easy to implement, and with the exception of salary adjustments, had no monetary costs attached.[20] The survey results were presented at a library-wide town meeting, and in the winter of 2005/06, the AUL and the associate director of MIS held open sessions with staff to review the results of the surveys and focus groups in depth. This was another way to collect feedback from staff as well as to let them know what had happened as a result of their input. Other metrics were eventually added to our Scorecard for which the worklife survey provided data. MIS and Library Human Resources have continued to field the worklife survey every other spring.

Sustainable Assessment

Part of the MIS mission is to help staff understand how using data can improve their success and improve service to our users. We present survey results at library town meetings and have held classes in basic statistical concepts. All MIS staff members serve on numerous library committees and groups and use reports to those groups to help educate staff. We also offer our services for particular projects or answer questions from staff about studies we have done. During 2005/06, MIS staff members attended staff meetings with the twenty-three departments that existed in the library at the time. We presented targeted data from our annual statistical report, the staff worklife survey, and the user survey, to show how data could be used by a department, and what kind of services MIS could offer them.

As part of our library's mandate to share our ideas and experiences with others in the profession, Jim Self, with Steve Hiller of the University of Washington Libraries, founded "ESP: Effective, Sustainable, and Practical Library Assessment," an ARL program supporting sustainable assessment in libraries.[21] Between 2005 and 2010, Self and Hiller traveled to over forty participating libraries across North America and abroad, to analyze where each was in its assessment program and offer advice on how to improve it. Each library that participated in the analysis received a report and recommendations. The program continues today and demonstrates the importance of a library's leadership, of a library staff devoted to users, and of a supportive organizational culture to ensure the success of assessment programs. Self, with the U.Va Library, ARL, and the University of Washington Libraries, is also an organizer of the Library Assessment Conference, which has been held biannually since 2006.

Another contribution of the U.Va Library to the library assessment community was a 2007 ARL SPEC Kit that studied the state of library assessment in ARL libraries.[22] Written by the associate MIS director and Stephanie Wright of the University of Washington Libraries, this project surveyed seventy-three ARL libraries, asking questions about their assessment methods, history, activities, organizational structure, distribution and use of results, training and professional development, and library assessment culture. It was apparent from the study that assessment programs were pervasive in North American libraries at this time and that the assessment experience at U.Va was not very different from that of libraries across the continent.

Conclusion

One MIS goal is to foster a culture of assessment at the library. In all of the ways outlined above, we believe this has been accomplished. Asking our users for input is now our first thought rather than our last. For example, in 2007/08 we were mandated to renovate space in our undergraduate library to accommodate the use of student laptops, rather than library- or university-provided desktops. A task force analyzed data on actual usage of the desktops from the information technology division and data from the university's annual technology survey of students. The task force also did a quick paper survey to determine what uses students made of laptops and desktops in the library. With assistance from the User Requirements/Usability Community, focus groups/brainstorming sessions were held to gain student input on their needs for laptop or mobile computing.[23] Results indicated that the environment of the library *in general* was very important to students who spent many of their waking hours there. The students were happy to offer suggestions for comfortable furniture and aesthetic elements as well as to contribute ideas for redesigning the area. In less than a year, the study was completed and the space was refurbished.

In 2008/09, MIS performed interviews with all library departments to inventory what kinds of assessment were being done. This inventory confirmed that gathering and using data and user input was now pervasive throughout the library. In general, technical units collected data on library operations and public service units gathered opinions and ideas from users.

Originally a committee and then a three-person department, MIS now works closely with the user experience librarian, the User Requirements/ Usability Community, various members of the library administration, and other appropriate staff members to continue its work of gathering, analyzing, and interpreting library data of various kinds. The data are used by staff and managers to make effective changes in the library's programs that enhance our users' experience of the library. We have been fortunate to be able to extend hours for the undergraduate library to twenty-four hours a day, five days a week; increase the speed with which newly ordered books are made available to users; and create a study space for graduate students in the main library. Acquiring the additional resources to make these and other improvements for our users from an already strained university budget would not have been possible without data from our users and internal studies to support our requests.

NOTES

1. Robert E. Molyneux, *The Gerould Statistics 1907/08-1961/62*, 2nd ed. (Washington, DC: Association of Research Libraries, 1998), table 1, http://fisher.lib.virginia.edu/libsites/gerould/data/virginia.html.
2. "A Tribute to Kendon Lee Stubbs," University of Virginia Library, 2009, www.lib.virginia.edu/kls/text_only.html.
3. Kendon Stubbs, "University Libraries: Standards and Statistics," *College & Research Libraries* 42 (November 1981): 528–38.
4. Kendon Stubbs et al., "The ARL Library Index and Quantitative Relationships in the ARL: A Report" (Washington, DC: Association of Research Libraries, 1980), www.arl.org/bm~doc/stubbs80.pdf; and Jim Self, "Library Assessment Award Remarks for Kendon Stubbs," October 25, 2010, http://libraryassessment.org/bm~doc/assessment_award_kendon_stubbs.pdf.
5. Jim Self, "Library Assessment Award Remarks."
6. Ibid.
7. University of Virginia, University Committees, Thomas Jefferson Awards Committee, 2011, www.virginia.edu/universitycommittees/TJaward/

tja_charge.html. See also "University Confers Its Highest Honor on Kendon Stubbs, University Library Innovator," 1998, www.lib.virginia.edu/old-press/98-99/stubbs2.html; and John T. Casteen, "Kendon Lee Stubbs: Citation upon the Presentation of the Thomas Jefferson Award," October 30, 1998, www.lib.virginia.edu/old-press/98-99/kendon.pdf.

8. University of Virginia Library, Management Information Services, "1993 Faculty Survey–Questionnaire," 1993, www2.lib.virginia.edu/mis/reports/facsurv93/fac93.html.

9. Lynda S. White, ed., *Surveying Our Users: The University of Virginia Libraries*, (Charlottesville: University of Virginia Library, 1998–2011), www2.lib.virginia.edu/mis/reports/.

10. Jim Self, "1993 Baseline Study," University of Virginia Library, 1996, www2.lib.virginia.edu/mis/reports/BaselineREV.pdf.

11. Steve Hiller and James Self, "From Measurement to Management: Using Statistics Wisely in Planning and Decision-Making," *Library Trends* 53 (Summer 2004): 146.

12. Lynda S. White, "A Service Quality Survey at the University of Virginia Library, 1998," www2.lib.virginia.edu/mis/reports/SERVQUALReport1998.pdf.

13. Vicki Coleman et al., "Toward a TQM Paradigm: Using SERVQUAL to Measure Library Service Quality," *College & Research Libraries* 58 (May 1997): 237–49.

14. Jim Self, "Bound for Disappointment: Faculty and Journals at Research Institutions," *ARL: A Bimonthly Report* 257 (April 2008), 9, www.arl.org/bm~doc/arl-br-257-bound.pdf.

15. Jennifer Rutner and Jim Self, "Still Bound for Disappointment? Another Look at Faculty and Library Journal Collections," in *Proceedings of the 2010 Library Assessment Conference: Building Effective, Sustainable, Practical Assessment, October 24–27, 2010, Baltimore, Maryland* (Washington, DC: Association of Research Libraries, 2011), 297–309. http://libraryassessment.org/bm~doc/proceedings-lac-2010.pdf.

16. Lynda S. White, "Benchmarking Team Report on the Shelving Process," 1999, www2.lib.virginia.edu/mis/benchmarking/ShelvingReport.pdf; and "Report on the Benchmarking Process," 1999, www2.lib.virginia.edu/mis/benchmarking/benchmarking_process_rept.html.

17. Lynda S. White, ed., *University of Virginia Library Statistics Report* (Charlottesville: University of Virginia Library, 2001–2011), www2.lib.virginia.edu/mis/statistics/.

18. Robert S. Kaplan and David P. Norton, "The Balanced Scorecard—Measures That Drive Performance," *Harvard Business Review* 70, no. 1 (1992): 71–79; and Robert S. Kaplan and David P. Norton, *The Balanced Scorecard: Translating Strategy into Action* (Boston: Harvard Business School Press, 1996).

19. Molly Royse et al., "Charting a Course for Diversity: An Experience in Climate Assessment," *portal: Libraries and the Academy* 6 (January 2006): 23–45, http://muse.jhu.edu/journals/portal_libraries_and_the_academy/ v006/6.1royse.html.
20. Yolanda Cooper, "Worklife Survey and Focus Groups," 2005, www2.lib .virginia.edu/mis/reports/worklife2004/ResponsesHandout.pdf.
21. Association of Research Libraries, "Effective, Sustainable, and Practical Library Assessment," 2011, www.arl.org/stats/initiatives/esp/.
22. Stephanie Wright and Lynda S. White, *SPEC Kit 303: Library Assessment* (Washington, DC: Association of Research Libraries, 2007), www.arl.org/ bm~doc/spec303web.pdf.
23. Donna Tolson and Matt Ball, "What If We Don't Provide Computers?: Assessment for Reduction," *Proceedings of the 2008 Library Assessment Conference: Building Effective, Sustainable, Practical Assessment, August 4–7, 2008, Seattle, Washington* (Washington, DC: Association of Research Libraries, 2009), 238, http://libraryassessment.org/bm~doc/proceedings-lac-2008.pdf.

CHESTALENE PINTOZZI
University of Arizona Libraries

3
The Implementation and Evolution of Quality Management in the University of Arizona Libraries

E STABLISHED IN 1885, THE UNIVERSITY OF ARIZONA (UA) IS A public, comprehensive, land grant, AAU, Research I university located in Tucson, Arizona. As of fall 2011, UA offered 300 undergraduate and graduate degrees through twenty colleges and eleven schools on three campuses serving 29,719 undergraduates, 6,962 graduate students, and 1,376 professional and medical students. The University of Arizona Libraries are the primary libraries serving all UA colleges except the College of Law and the Colleges of Medicine, Pharmacy, Nursing, and Public Health, which are served by separate Law and Health Sciences Libraries.

This chapter will discuss the implementation and evolution of quality approaches in the University of Arizona Libraries over the past twenty years. During this time the library has transformed into a fully team-based organization with an emphasis on continual learning and data-based decision making. The organization has engaged in three major organizational restructurings— the first implemented in 1993, the second implemented in 2008, and the third implemented in 2011—and several small-scale reorganizations between 1993 and 2008 that have directly or indirectly affected the implementation and use of quality approaches and tools.

To provide context, at the end of the 1980s the University of Arizona Libraries were an excellent, but very traditional, collections-focused, hierarchical organization. After the longtime university library director retired in 1990, the interim library director and the library's leadership group recognized the need to explore ways in which the libraries could best meet the information needs of its users in a rapidly changing, financially constrained environment. An Access/Ownership Task Force was appointed to undertake this analysis and make recommendations. This group concluded in 1991 that the libraries could not continue business as usual by focusing on building collections designed to locally meet as many needs as possible, but instead needed to move to a mix of access and ownership. In addition, the report noted that the structure of the libraries, designed around the acquisition and processing of library materials, would need to change to support the new work of access.[1]

A new university librarian (title later changed to dean of libraries) was appointed in July 1991 and was immediately faced with a budget cut resulting from reductions in the university's state funding allocation. After review of the Access/Ownership report, consultation with other UA library administrators, and consultation with the director of the Office of Management Services (OMS) of the Association of Research Libraries (ARL), she initiated a process to redesign the University of Arizona Libraries to address the needs and changes identified by the task force and the broader challenges and changes facing academic research libraries.

Introducing Quality Management and Process Improvement

The University of Arizona Libraries does not have a formal quality program. Instead the design and focus of the organization embody core elements of Total Quality Management (TQM)—customer satisfaction, continuous improvement, empowerment, and teamwork. The libraries' principles of customer focus, continuous improvement and learning, diversity, integrity, and flexibility reflect these elements.[2] While the libraries now has only one position partially allocated to formally support assessment, responsibility for implementing quality approaches and assessment is deeply embedded in and distributed throughout the organization. All library employees are expected to understand, support, and learn the skills required to apply the libraries' principles.

ARL staff began exploring Total Quality Management in the early 1990s.[3] The OMS consultant engaged by the libraries for the 1992/93 restructuring introduced some general TQM approaches during the ensuing sixteen-month organizational redesign process.[4] The result was a customer-focused, team-based, flattened organizational structure. Assessing and analyzing needs of the library's customers became high-priority work for all teams across the organization and was expected to drive decision making.[5] Staff training and learning were recognized as key components required for the organization to succeed. Two key positions were allocated to support this initiative—an assistant dean for facilitation (later retitled assistant dean for team and organization development) and an assistant to the dean for staff development, diversity, and recruitment.[6]

In 1991 the university began a TQM initiative titled Continuous Organizational Renewal (CORe) in partnership with and utilizing the services of an executive from Intel Corporation.[7] Shortly after the libraries' restructuring, the UA provost directed all academic units to implement strategic planning groups and to develop strategic plans following the State of Arizona's Management by Planning (MBP) method. In 1993/94 the libraries' first Strategic Long Range Planning Team was appointed and charged with scanning the environment, articulating the libraries' vision and mission, developing three- to five-year goals and strategies, and managing the identification of priority projects with indicators, later called performance measures. The process employed in the libraries combined elements of the state's MBP approach and the approach used by Intel that was based on the principles of Hoshin Planning.

Measures of progress toward goals included input, output, outcomes, quality, and efficiency. Figure 3.1 provides some examples of quality-based measures included in the Libraries' 1994/95 Strategic Plan.

Among the areas targeted for improvement in the 1994/95 Annual Plan were three projects that became the first process improvement (PI) efforts in the libraries. They focused on the problem areas of reshelving, interlibrary

FIGURE 3.1

Examples of Performance and Quality Standards, 2002–2006

Strategy	Indicator	Goal
To expedite physical access to collections.	Satisfied customers.	Assessment tools indicate 25% increase in customer satisfaction by 1996.
To provide effective access to local and remote resources through electronic non-mediated services.	Services meet customer needs.	Assessment tools indicate 10% increase in customer satisfaction each year.
To provide educational programs and services for U of A undergraduate and graduate students.	Ability to use resources and services.	Assessment tools indicate 10% increase in user ability

loan, and reserves processing. Work in these areas was not meeting customer expectations and was slow and costly, resulting in a negative effect on customer satisfaction. The libraries applied for and received a $24,000 Council on Library Resources grant to hire a process improvement consultant and provide support for the three process improvement teams. The reshelving project team (PITCrew) was the first trained and the first to fully implement formal process improvement. The team was very successful at dramatically decreasing turnaround time for reshelving from an average of forty-nine hours to an average of four hours, saving over $30,000 a year.[8] This project and the process improvement projects that followed—including reserves, photocopying, and technical services—carefully followed the PDCA (Plan, Do, Check, Act) model, the foundation of most quality programs.[9]

After 1999, the libraries experienced some loss of leadership and of staff with process improvement knowledge and skill, diminishing the effectiveness of initial improvements and the ability of new PI teams to implement changes. No new PI teams were formed from 2000 to 2005. In 2005 concerns over these losses drove the libraries to send a staff member to a workshop to learn the Six Sigma/DMAIC approach to process improvement. Assessment of this approach resulted in the training of additional staff in the libraries. The Process Improvement Resources Group (PIRG), a group of Six Sigma/DMAIC-trained staff, was then formed to assist with new process improvement projects.[10]

One such project was Finding Information in a New Landscape (FINL). FINL team members used the PIRG to help them rigorously apply process improvement tools to reference and information desk services. This was the first project in the libraries that focused primarily on work that was done mostly by librarians. The results of the assessment of this process demonstrated that a high percentage of questions asked at the reference and information desks did not require the knowledge and skills of librarians. Although there was some internal controversy, particularly among librarians, regarding the methodology and analysis, the outcome of this assessment resulted in removing librarians from all but one service desk and replacing them with carefully trained classified staff. This freed up librarians' time to focus on high-level work requiring professional expertise.[11]

The PIRG also advised and supported process improvement projects for interlibrary loan (ILL) article borrowing, recruitment and hiring, and materials check-in. Cost savings from these projects ranged from $3,100 to $10,000 per year. The ILL process improvement project also significantly increased the three-day fill rate for articles requested by UA Libraries' customers from 45 percent to 69 percent.[12]

The next major step in integrating quality approaches across the libraries was the development of the Performance Effectiveness Management System

(PEMS). This system was designed by a library project team with the assistance of local consultants. The result was a measure-based approach that integrated and aligned team planning and development of personal goals with the libraries' strategic plan.[13] In the PEMS process, each functional (permanent) team follows a planning process that includes articulation or review of the team's vision and mission, and assessment and analysis of the needs of the team's customers. Teams then identify their mission-critical processes and develop performance measures and quality standards that reflect desired outcomes for customers, financial benefits to stakeholders, efficiency of internal processes, and/or staff gains through learning band growth. This process is based on the Balanced Scorecard model articulated by Robert S. Kaplan and David P. Norton.[14] The next steps include the development of strategies and projects that will advance the libraries' goals, better meet known customer needs, or improve critical processes, followed by the development of performance measures and quality standards for the work of the team.[15]

Individuals then develop personal goals for the year that are aligned with their team's and the libraries' goals and strategies. Peer developmental review teams are formed for each individual to provide feedback and advice on his or her progress toward the year's goals, performance measures, and quality standards. Individual goals include learning goals to continue developing the libraries' capacity to effectively and efficiently accomplish new and changed work. Employee evaluations are performed by functional team leaders. These evaluations are informed by feedback from peer groups and the functional team leader's own assessment of the individual's work during the year. The libraries later implemented a career progression, merit-based approach to pay increases, to reward learning and the application of learning to benefit customers.[16]

Performance measures and quality standards were developed for almost all critical processes and projects in the libraries by the end of the 1990s. For example, turnaround time was a key measure for reshelving, ILL, and reserves processing as well as for placing book orders, checking in periodicals, and other similar work. Customer satisfaction was measured by locally developed surveys. Examples included a survey of interlibrary loan customers to determine if they were satisfied with turnaround time. Another survey queried faculty regarding the percentage of their information needs that were met by the libraries and their satisfaction with turnaround times.

Introduction of LibQUAL and Action Gap Surveys

When Fred Heath and Colleen Cook of Texas A&M University collaborated with ARL in 1999 to adapt SERVQUAL to measure library service quality, the

University of Arizona Libraries participated in the beta testing. Impressed with the results, the libraries subsequently chose to conduct the resulting LIBQUAL survey annually from 2001 to the present. LibQUAL provides an opportunity to systematically measure service quality against customer expectations and assess customer satisfaction. In 2002 the libraries began to develop and use performance measures and quality standards based on LibQUAL results.

The advantage of utilizing LibQUAL over locally developed surveys lies in the fact that the methodology was fully tested and validated and thus provides reliable results for measuring and reporting progress to the university administration and to inform library units. The libraries are currently using five performance measures and quality standards based on LibQUAL dimensions and local questions. (See figure 3.2.)

With the construction of an Integrated Learning Center in 2000/01, however, it became clear that an additional approach was needed to assess service quality and customer satisfaction. The Integrated Learning Center included an Information Commons (IC) focused on undergraduates. To identify, from a

FIGURE 3.2

Examples of 2012 Performance Measures and
Quality Standards Based on LibQUAL

3–5 Year Measure	Quality Standard
Decrease in the mean difference between desired and perceived service for all UA respondents to the LibQUAL "Information Control" dimension.	Reduce superiority gap from –1.09 (average 2005–07) to –0.87 measured in 2012.
Decrease in the mean difference between desired and perceived service for all UA respondents to the LibQUAL "Affect of Service" dimension.	Reduce superiority gap from –0.87 (average 2005–07) to –0.70 measured in 2012.
Decrease in the mean difference between desired and perceived service for all UA respondents to the LibQUAL "Personalization features in the electronic library" question.	Reduce superiority gap from –0.81 measured in 2007 to –0.65 measured in 2012.
Decrease in the mean difference between desired and perceived service for all UA students to the LibQUAL question: "Teaching me how to access, evaluate, and use information."	Reduce LibQUAL superiority gap by x % from baseline measured in 2009–11 by 2014. (*Note: % will be determined once baseline is established.*)
Decrease in the mean difference between desired and perceived service for all UA respondents to the LibQUAL "Library as Place" dimension.	Reduce superiority gap from –0.93 (average 2005–07) to –0.75 measured in 2012.

customer perspective, how well the IC was meeting customer needs, an internally developed Action Gap Survey was designed. This survey was later titled the Library Services Survey and is still in use today. Survey questions address library facilities, assistance finding information resources and answers to questions, access to digitized materials, and customers' waiting time to get help. Results are analyzed primarily by the Access and Information Services Team (AIST), which is responsible for addressing significant gaps identified by the survey in the team's annual strategic planning process.

Restructuring, Project Management, Assessment, and Strategic Planning

Two major organizational restructurings—in 2008 and in 2011—and several smaller restructurings have occurred since the first major organizational redesign and major restructuring in 1993. Each has been driven by specific forces such as changing customer needs, the need to incorporate new or changed work, and, in the 2008 restructuring, by campus budget cuts. What has remained constant throughout each restructuring is the organization's commitment to its team-based and customer-focused approach, to the general principles of quality management, and to its values of customer focus, continuous learning, accountability, flexibility, and diversity. The current organizational structure consists of only nine teams. The libraries' staff is also much smaller, with only 138 filled professional and support positions in 2011 as compared to 227 in 1991.

While the libraries does not have a formal quality program, there have been personnel changes over the past twenty years that support quality approaches. During the 1993 restructuring, for instance, an assistant dean for team facilitation was created. This position was later changed to assistant dean for team and organizational development and charged with serving as a quality advisor to teams and with supporting quality initiatives. A subsequent review and reclassification of staff, undertaken apart from the organizational restructurings, resulted in several positions being designated as information analysts. Individuals in these positions are responsible for supporting environmental scanning, data collection and analysis, and ongoing monitoring of processes and quality standards for their teams.

As more of the libraries' strategic work was assigned to project teams over the years, with significantly fewer staff available to accomplish the work, it became apparent in 2008 that improvements in our project planning and management processes were needed. The dean of libraries and the retiring assistant dean for team and organizational development selected Ernie Nielsen, managing director of Enterprise Services Portfolio Management at Brigham

Young University (BYU), to train a selected cohort of twenty-five staff in his approach to project management. Over the next two years the libraries contracted with Nielsen to train approximately seventy-five more staff members. The BYU approach is designed to closely align organizational projects with the organization's priorities, and help prioritize, select, and sequence projects to optimize limited resources.[17]

The director of project management and assessment position was created following the 2008 restructuring. This individual is responsible for training staff; supporting project sponsors, project managers, and project teams; and monitoring projects to ensure that projects make effective use of resources and are completed in a timely manner. A Cabinet subgroup, the Portfolio Management Group, was also created to monitor resources available for projects, to review proposed projects for strategic value, to prioritize projects, and to make recommendations regarding project approval to the Cabinet.

The libraries' approach to strategic planning has also evolved. The Strategic Long Range Planning Team (SLRP) now reviews and revises the strategic plan each year, changing goals and strategies only when the need for change is clearly evident in the results of the environmental scan. Strategic projects may emerge from dialogue among SLRP, the Library Cabinet, and the Portfolio Management Group; from teams' annual planning; or from proposals put forward by individuals or groups at any time during the year. In the last two years, most strategic projects have evolved through the team strategic planning process, with review and feedback from the Cabinet and the Portfolio Management Group. The libraries' three- to five-year strategic plan is shaped by an environmental scan, including review of customer needs, changes, and trends. Organizational progress toward goals and objectives is measured by a set of library-wide performance measures and quality standards, as well as by team and individual goals, performance measures, and quality standards.

Strategic projects are designed and expected to result in significant progress toward fulfilling goals in the libraries' strategic plan. The Portfolio Management Group assesses proposals for new strategic projects against a set of questions designed to measure how well the proposal supports the libraries' strategic plan, the university's strategic plan, and optimization of resources, processes, or productivity. This approach is based on the BYU project prioritization method.[18]

Annual strategic frameworks developed by functional teams are aligned with the libraries' strategic plan and include team projects, performance measures, and quality standards. Teams report progress to the Cabinet three times each year. In the two most recent years the Cabinet, SLRP, and the PMG have jointly reviewed and given feedback on proposed team and strategic projects.

Current State of Quality in the Libraries

The University of Arizona Libraries has integrated general quality principles into all facets of the organization. The organization is deeply committed to assessment of customer needs and to data-driven strategic planning and decision making. Improving environmental scanning and assessment of the needs of UA faculty, students, and researchers is a high priority that emerged from the 2011 restructuring. Commitment to assessment was demonstrated by the creation of the position of director of project management and assessment in 2008, by the ongoing collection and analysis of large quantities of data and information, and by the implementation of the positions of information analyst on several teams. Decisions by the Cabinet and by functional and cross-functional teams are data-driven or at least data-informed.

While fewer process improvement projects have been undertaken in recent years, several teams continue to monitor performance in areas that have undergone process improvement. Some teams also monitor volume of work, to inform staffing models and the allocation of resources within the team and across the libraries. For example, the Delivery, Description and Acquisitions Team has quality standards establishing turnaround time for processing new materials at ten days from receipt and turnaround time for delivering articles requested by customers at twenty-four hours. Further, 95 percent of catalog records for special format materials must be created within forty-eight hours. Although few new staff have been trained in process improvement, at least two team leaders and several staff members have a deep knowledge of process improvement and provide support as needed.

The gradual implementation of the concept of product management is a recent development. Selected library services are designated as products, and product managers are assigned to develop and manage a road map, or plan, for the service. This approach also includes principles of quality management. Each product must be justified based on customer needs. Road maps for products are expected to include a plan for assessing the quality of the product or its value to customers and a plan for improvement if quality is not satisfactory.

Ongoing assessment of service quality is recognized as critical to the success of the libraries and is integrated throughout the system. Assessment of student learning and development of critical thinking, for example, are high priorities for the university administration. The Instructional Services Team has been charged with implementing the use of formal methodologies to access the effectiveness of tutorials, tools, and credit courses developed by the libraries. Assessment was built into the one-credit, undergraduate Online Research Lab course, to measure student learning using pretests and posttests. A recent research study comparing students taking the online course to those receiving standard instruction showed students taking the online course demonstrated greater learning.[19]

Assessment of customer satisfaction continues to be central to the libraries' quality initiatives and has become more important with the libraries' increased dependence on student fees. LibQUAL comments are analyzed to better understand rankings at the domain and question level, and to identify issues of concern to segments of the libraries' customers.[20] Both the Strategic Long Range Planning Team and functional teams use this information to inform planning. The Library Services Survey is now conducted in the Information Commons areas of the Main, Science-Engineering, and Fine Arts libraries and in Special Collections to assess and better understand the needs of customers who are physically present in those spaces. Because most of these users are students, the results are particularly useful in determining what improvements they want and what they feel the libraries are doing well.

In the area of information resources management, the libraries have set selection effectiveness quality standards for indexing and abstracting services, electronic journals, print journals, and monographs based on use and other factors. Patron Driven Access (PDA), which is locally called On-Demand Information Delivery, was implemented in 2011. One measure of success built into this system is the turnaround time from order to delivery for print books. A strategic project team has been appointed and charged with developing and implementing additional measures and quality standards for PDA by the end of 2011/12. The allocation of the libraries' materials budget is data-driven, using selected statistics representing customer needs.[21]

Support for staff training and development has remained a high priority since the initial 1993 restructuring. All UA Libraries employees are eligible for twenty-four days of professional leave each year. The libraries continue to provide partial funding for professional and staff travel, although the university has eliminated central funding and prohibits use of state funds for this purpose. Training continues to be supported through both a library-allocated training fund and through a component of the PEMS process that focuses on identifying staff training needs.

Results of the University of Arizona Libraries' Focus on Quality

Although the libraries' budget has been cut numerous times over the past twenty years during general university budget reductions, the libraries have also received significant support from the university administration. The libraries' materials budget has been exempt from cuts for the past ten years.

In part, this is due to the effectiveness with which the libraries have managed this budget and have demonstrated the value UA customers receive from library resources. The university has allocated funding for ongoing equipment refresh costs and overnight staffing for the Information Commons in the Main Library. Requests to fill library positions are almost always approved, although there have been several university hiring freezes in the past decade. The university recently approved the libraries' request to offer credit courses. This was particularly significant because the university is implementing a version of responsibility-centered management, in which tuition income is partially distributed to academic units based on student credit hours taught.

Both UA student organizations, the Associated Students of the University of Arizona and the Graduate and Professional Students Council, supported the implementation of a student library fee that was first used to support new services. As state budget cuts and subsequent UA budget cuts continued, the students have also supported a subsequent fee increase to help maintain existing services.

Overall faculty satisfaction with information resources has increased, as measured by the LibQUAL Information Access dimension. Because of effective management of the materials budget, the libraries have been able to migrate 97 percent of serials subscriptions to electronic format and to provide rapid delivery of materials through interlibrary loan. Satisfaction with library services as measured by the LibQUAL Affect of Service dimension has also improved. Cost savings from process improvement and funding from the new student library fees have enabled the libraries to continue to provide high-quality services and to implement new services as budgets and staffing levels have been cut in the libraries as well as across campus.

The Future of Quality in the University of Arizona Libraries

The University of Arizona Libraries are less than a year into implementation of the 2011 organizational restructuring, with a workforce that is much smaller and with processes that are vastly different from those that existed twenty years ago. The library now focuses on online instruction rather than face-to-face in-classroom instruction, on just-in-time customer-driven delivery of both electronic and print content rather than on collection building, on electronic delivery of as many resources and services as possible rather than on print materials and in-person assistance, and on re-purposing space to accommodate customer needs rather than on maintaining space designed for the libraries' convenience.

To effectively demonstrate value to our multiple constituencies, the libraries' performance measures and quality standards must continue to evolve.

At the present time, the libraries collect, compile, and assess well over 200 measures library-wide that are used by the libraries' nine functional and three standing cross-functional teams. Decisions related to the selection and retention of serials, for example, are driven by a number of factors including use, citations, and other demonstrated customer need. Staffing models for several teams require data documenting the volume of work and the average time needed to accomplish required tasks, to identify the full-time equivalents needed to accomplish their work. Several teams utilize the analysis of LibQUAL survey results and comments to identify areas in the greatest need of improvement.

Some of the libraries' current measures, data, and information may not be applicable or needed in the future. Some are not currently being used or are not being used effectively. It is understood that new or revised measures will be needed to assess the quality and value of new or changed library services and resources. New or revised measures may be required to meet new or changed standards or requirements of the Arizona Board of Regents, the university administration, and the Arizona governor and legislature.

An assessment plan for the libraries was drafted before the 2011 restructuring began, but work was suspended pending expected changes in the organization. A goal for 2011/12 is to revise and complete a coordinated plan for assessment across the library system. A recently completed project addressing the value of the libraries yielded recommendations that need to be incorporated into an assessment plan. Furthermore, Cabinet, functional team leaders, and the Strategic Long Range Planning Team need to be engaged in a process to review, assess, and inform a three- to five-year plan for assessing the quality of services and resources, assessing and monitoring the effectiveness and cost-effectiveness of processes, and demonstrating value to campus stakeholders.

The economic recovery in Arizona is expected to be very slow, and it is likely that the state's universities will experience additional budget cuts or have flat budgets for the next several years or longer. The University of Arizona is unlikely to receive funding increases under proposed changes to the university's funding formula. A scenario planning process to develop a new long-term strategic plan for the university has begun. The environmental scan and assessment of driving forces indicate that UA must make major changes to be successful in the future. The libraries will, no doubt, be affected by these upcoming changes. The Arizona Board of Regents and the state legislature are widely expected to adopt a performance-driven allocation process for state funds. The libraries have become more dependent on student fees and will need to request a significant increase in the next few years if current services are to be maintained. The current strategy of continuing to seek increases in the student fee as library costs increase in the future may prove problematic as concerns about tuition and fees increase. Student support for higher fees is heavily dependent on the libraries' ability to understand and meet their evolving needs and demonstrate results to UA's student governance and advisory groups.

Challenges

Perhaps the libraries' greatest challenge has been identifying and designing appropriate outcome measures. It is much easier to measure inputs and outputs—the number of books and journals received, the number of questions asked, the number of students in a class, the number of classes taught, the number of items circulated, or the number of downloads of electronic resources—than to measure the results of the customers' use of the libraries' services and resources.

Another major challenge has been staff's perceived conflict between quality and efficiency. Budget cuts and resulting staff reductions created an environment in which additional resources were unavailable for needed quality improvements. This required staff to look beyond assumptions that the solution to low quality was to add more staff or pay more for faster service. It also required staff to question their own assumptions about how quality was defined, to learn how customers define it, and to design work to match customer expectations rather than their own beliefs and values.

Maintaining a focus on representative and reliable data rather than on complaints from squeaky wheels and anecdotal evidence is also difficult. A complaint from a faculty acquaintance, from a department head, or an unhappy student at an information desk presents a personal face that, for many staff, tends to be more compelling than data showing a high level of satisfaction with our information resources and with our quality of service. The individual comments from LibQUAL, the libraries' customer feedback mechanism, and focus groups also feel more personal and therefore more important to many staff. Approaches that have helped include the discussion and use of Balanced Scorecard concepts or a simple triangulation of sources, rather than relying on solely one source of information. Carefully collected and analyzed quantitative information can be more compelling when used in combination with selected qualitative data. This approach can make a strong case stronger by combining statistical evidence with individual stories.

Efficient and accurate compilation of data and effective reporting are difficult. Required data and information come from many discrete sources, and no one individual has access to all of the systems from which data are pulled. Similar data from multiple similar sources may not be truly comparable. The libraries are currently in the process of implementing a commercial system to manage and archive our data and generate reports. The goal is to improve accuracy by reducing the handling and reformatting of data, and to increase analysis and reporting options to help staff better understand and communicate results. Useful information comes from multiple sources. Connections to and two-way communication with stakeholders must be developed and maintained to obtain up-to-date, useful information about the campus environment and trends and the changing needs of library customers.

A final challenge is the difficulty of assessing complex systems and the work of library faculty. Developing and gathering data on quality and outcome measures for work such as the design and implementation of an online course requires approaches that are more sophisticated than developing a quality standard for the turnaround time for a book order. An added problem is the inaccurate assumption by some library faculty that all aspects of their work are protected by academic freedom and that it is inappropriate to measure or apply process improvement to it. This challenge is complicated by concerns about potential requirements for accountability and the sometimes unacknowledged fear that the results of assessment may reflect negatively on and be used against individuals engaged in professional work.

Conclusions

It is becoming more and more critical for academic libraries to understand the needs and expectations of the library's primary user groups and key stakeholders. The University of Arizona Libraries' primary customers are defined as the students, faculty, and staff of the university and the specific scholarly and research communities served by the Center for Creative Photography and Special Collections. Key stakeholders include the university president, provost, Faculty Senate, and other governance groups, including the Associated Students of the University of Arizona and the Graduate and Professional Students Council.

Customer and stakeholder needs and expectations can often be discerned through analysis of existing information, through direct communication with selected individuals, and by analysis of trends in survey results. It is essential to select measures that best provide cost-effective ways of assessing progress toward goals and customer satisfaction. While triangulation of representative, reliable data is the best approach, surrogate data may prove useful in some cases. For example, use of electronic resources can demonstrate, to a certain extent, their value to customers. Anecdotal evidence and qualitative measures used wisely and in conjunction with quantitative data will result in better understanding and increased likelihood of improved results. One problem or concern raised by a few vociferous customers does not create a trend. While an immediate issue often must be addressed, before making any major changes it is important to carefully analyze what is known, find facts, and make a data-driven decision.

As accrediting organizations and funding bodies in higher education demand greater accountability in general, it has become more important than ever to measure outcomes and demonstrate results. It is critical to first understand clearly why a particular service is being offered. Then explore options for assessing baseline performance and changes resulting from additions to or improvements to the service. Many universities and accrediting bodies are placing increased emphasis on improving student learning outcomes, making it important for academic libraries to be able to demonstrate results for their instruction and information literacy initiatives.

Time and effort must be allocated to exploring and understanding why the library is not meeting customer expectations or organizational quality standards. Processes must be studied to identify root causes of delays, changes must be developed to address those causes, solutions must be tested, results must be analyzed, and processes must be tweaked and then tested again. Libraries must not rely on personal or organizational assumptions about what causes problems and what needs to be done. Likewise libraries should not rely on "standard practices" unless there is clear evidence from benchmarking or other systematic analysis that those practices yield good results.

Tracking progress and trends in critical areas must be an ongoing effort. It is not necessary or desirable to continuously measure all activities, but it is important to identify services that are most important to customers and to sample frequently enough to identify gaps or problems in performance. It is very useful to develop and follow an assessment plan that coordinates assessment activities across the organization. Follow-up is critical. Assessment is useless unless the results are used to assess performance, identify gaps in performance, and then develop and implement improvements. While it is not possible to achieve perfection or please all customers and stakeholders, constant progress can be made.

Academic libraries must learn the needs of their customers and know how their institution defines success. It is necessary to have a clear vision describing the desired results of the library's resources and services before implementing a quality or assessment infrastructure. Libraries must develop and maintain a clear understanding of why new services were created and of the value added by old services. Keeping the big picture in mind and understanding that an academic research library is a large entity with interrelated and interdependent entities help provide perspective and inform strategic planning. It is critical to maintain awareness that changing one entity almost always affects another. As changes are implemented by the library or when the environment changes, it is necessary to assess existing measures and quality standards and discontinue, revise, or replace them. This ongoing attention is needed to maintain a core set of measures that demonstrate the library's quality, value, and effectiveness. Academic libraries that expend the time and effort required to develop an effective quality program or embed quality or other similar principles into their organization will be better positioned to succeed in the future than those that do not.

NOTES

1. Douglas E. Jones et al., *Report of the Task Force on Access/Ownership Policy* (University of Arizona Library, ERIC Document 353 996, 1991).
2. University of Arizona Libraries, "Principles of the University of Arizona Libraries," www.library.arizona.edu/about/organization/principles.html.
3. Susan B. Bernard, *A Draft Model for Adopting Total Quality Management in a Research Library,* prepared for discussion at the American Library Association Midwinter Meeting, San Antonio, Texas, January 25, 1992 (Association of Research Libraries, Office of Management Services, 1992).
4. Susan Jurow, *Organizational Review and Design Project: Initial Meeting: Preliminary Outline* (Association of Research Libraries, Office of Management Services, 1992).
5. Laura J. Bender, "Team Organization-Learning Organization: The University of Arizona Four Years into It," *Information Outlook* 1, no. 9 (1997): 19–22.
6. Shelley E. Phipps and Joseph R. Diaz, "The Evolution of the Roles of Staff and Team Development in a Changing Organization: The University of Arizona Library Experience," in *Finding Common Ground: Creating the Library of the Future without Diminishing the Library of the Past,* ed. Cheryl LaGuardia and Barbara A. Mitchell (New York: Neal-Schuman, 1997).
7. Roger Caldwell, "The University of Arizona College of Agriculture and Life Sciences: A History from 1930 to 2010," University of Arizona, College of Agriculture and Life Sciences, 2011, http://cals.arizona.edu/pubs/general/az1543.pdf.
8. Shelley E. Phipps, "Data-Based Process Improvement in a Team-Based Learning Organization: Final Report to the Council on Library Resources on CLR 926," 1994.
9. Catharine A. Larson, "Customers First: Using Process Improvement to Improve Service Quality and Efficiency," *Reference Services Review* 26, no. 1 (1998): 51–60.
10. Shelley E. Phipps, "The Use of the Process Improvement DMAIC and Six Sigma Approaches to Improve Quality and Reduce Costs at the University of Arizona Library 1995–-2008" (unpublished, 2009).
11. Marianne Stowell Bracke et al., "Finding Information in a New Landscape: Developing New Service and Staffing Models for Mediated Information Services," *College & Research Libraries* 68, no. 3, (2007): 248–67.

12. Jeanne F. Voyles, Linda Dols, and Ellen Knight, "Interlibrary Loan Meets Six Sigma: The University of Arizona Library's Success Applying Process Improvement," *Journal of Interlibrary Loan, Document Delivery & Electronic Reserves* 19, no. 1 (2009): 75–94.

13. Shelley E. Phipps, "Performance Measurement as a Methodology for Assessing Team and Individual Performance: The University of Arizona Library Experience," in *Proceedings of the 3rd Northumbria International Conference on Performance Measurement in Libraries and Information Services* (Newcastle upon Tyne, Eng.: Information North, 2000): 113–17.

14. Robert S. Kaplan and David P. Norton, *The Balanced Scorecard* (Boston: Harvard Business School Press, 1996).

15. Carla Stoffle and Shelley Phipps, "Creating a Culture of Assessment: The University of Arizona Experience," *ARL: A Bimonthly Report on Research Library Issues & Actions* 230/231 (October/December 2003): 26–27.

16. Michael Ray, "Rewarding Strategic Learning and Performance: The Experience at the University of Arizona," *Library Administration & Management* 18, no. 3 (2004): 124–33.

17. Ernie Nielsen, "The Road to IT Governance Excellence," Pacific Edge Software White Paper, 2006, www.inst-informatica.pt/servicos/informacao -e-documentacao/biblioteca-digital/gestao-de-si-ti-1/it-governance/ RoadtoGovExcellence_WP_Fin.pdf.

18. Ibid.

19. Yvonne Mery, Jill Newby, and Ke Peng, "Why One-Shot Information Literacy Sessions Are Not the Future of Instruction: A Case for Online Credit Courses College & Research Libraries," *College & Research Libraries* 73, no. 4 (2012): 366–77.

20. Wendy Begay et al., "Quantifying Qualitative Data," *Journal of Library Administration* 40, no. 3/4 (2004): 111–19.

21. Patricia Promis, "Developing a Databased Budget Allocation Strategy: The University of Arizona Library Experience," *Collection Building* 15, no. 3 (1996): 5–9.

TERRIRUTH CARRIER
AND NANCY B. TURNER
Syracuse University Library

4
Committed to Quality

Syracuse University Library's
Program Management Center

ACADEMIC LIBRARIES ARE FACING AN INCREASED NEED TO redefine their value to their parent institutions. Traditional metrics do not adequately describe changing library collections and services. Today, academic libraries are functioning as more than repositories for physical collections and are moving toward purchasing, organizing, and delivering more digital resources. In 2008 Syracuse University's dean of libraries began to establish a set of more meaningful metrics that would demonstrate the library's value beyond its placement in the ranking of other Association of Research Libraries (ARL) libraries. Her goal was to have a more proactive assessment program, recognizing that additional data and a more sophisticated approach to its analysis were required.

Chartered in 1870 as a private, coeducational institution of higher education, Syracuse University is a leading research university in central New York State. It serves more than 20,000 full- and part-time students (14,671 undergraduate and 5,493 graduate students in fall 2011) from all 50 states and 90 countries, and has more than 1,158 faculty members. The library's diverse collections include more than 3.1 million volumes which are housed in multiple buildings throughout the campus. The library staff includes 6 administrators (dean, associate or assistant deans), 51 librarians, 35 professional and computer/technical staff, and 44 bargaining unit staff members.

The Program Management Center (PMC) resulted from the library administration's efforts to be more proactive in demonstrating value. The PMC is chartered with creating a library-wide system for improved data collection and processing, assessment and analysis, and quality control. The PMC recognized that the quality control approach had potential application to internal library processes as well as public services. Components of the Six Sigma and Project Management Professional methodologies, in particular, could successfully be applied to the library environment.[1] Thus, the basic flow of a PMC analysis is tightly entwined with that of the Six Sigma DMAIC approach: Define, Measure (benchmark), Analyze (investigate cause-and-effect relationships), Improve (automate and prototype), and Control (establish metrics for continuous monitoring). A project management approach to process improvement is also applied, helping staff to define workflows and processes, determine appropriate metrics, and continue to monitor and update metrics after a project's completion.

Assessment is now a critical component at each stage of a library project: at the beginning of each project to ensure appropriate and realistic goals are set and measured, in the middle to ensure the project is on target, and at the end to verify and ensure results are obtained. Any change in procedure, process, or service is captured and validated. Staff continues to monitor metrics throughout the life cycle of a process which operates beyond a project time line.

This chapter provides background information describing the creation of the PMC at Syracuse University and the responsibilities of the four individuals assigned to this department. It then describes two projects that demonstrate important aspects of the PMC approach at Syracuse. The Gate Count and Security Alarm project demonstrates a cross-departmental effort that involved the documentation of a process, the standardization of the process for data gathering, the development of a form that feeds into a web-enabled dashboard, and the ongoing monitoring of the collected data to ensure accuracy. The Library Measures Data Repository project demonstrates how Syracuse organizes, analyzes, and creates reports based on the data collected and makes it accessible to the appropriate audience.

Creating the Program Management Center

Prior to the organization of the PMC, assessment projects like LibQUAL were accomplished through library committees comprised of staff with expertise in assessment, data gathering, and statistics. The creation of the PMC reflects the library administration's need to support assessment more systematically, to find efficiencies in workflows, to use metrics effectively, and to redeploy staff to meet changing needs in an economic environment of decreasing resources. The new department provides leadership in organizing, monitoring, and managing projects. The PMC also provides leadership in assisting with project assessment, and ensuring that proper, meaningful metrics are identified and monitored. With the creation of the Program Management Center, led by a project management professional (PMP), the library realized the potential for promoting a project management methodology and quality approach.

With the creation of the PMC, the library's goals for quality and assessment were redefined. First, a project-oriented approach was employed to develop a continuous improvement mindset through the practice of assessment, process improvement, and streamlined workflows. Then data were used to advocate for appropriate budget, staff resources, and improved facilities. Next, focus turned toward educating the library staff on the new processes implemented and assessing improvements by monitoring metrics. Finally, a centralized database was developed consisting of information available to the library staff to support the management of library functions. The centralized database provides benchmarks, illustrates where improvements might be made, and provides more comparative data from other universities to advocate for the library at the institutional level.

The PMC supports the following functions: assessment; project management; workflows analysis; process improvements; software application development; metrics definition; data consolidation; analysis; and outcomes using the Project Management Professional Methodology and the Six Sigma approach to variance and workflow improvements. These functions were assigned to four positions, each requiring a specific yet complementary set of skills: research and assessment analyst; statistical and application analyst; program coordinator and data specialist; and director of program management.

The research and assessment analyst focuses on how the patron uses the library's services, facilities, and resources. The research analyst must possess analytical and detail-oriented skills, and understand all facets of the library, including the processes and procedures used by the library staff. An ability to understand how processes can be integrated across departments and to translate these processes into layman's terms is extremely important. The ability to communicate complex data in a variety of formats to be understood by internal and external audiences is also essential.

The application and statistical analyst ensures that large data sets are accessible in a format that allows data to be easily retrieved and analyzed, formatted for distribution, and archived. The application analyst utilizes Share-Point, the library's content management and internal communication tool, to develop applications that support library staff in their collection of data, to create dashboards for data visualization, and to identify potential trouble spots. Major responsibilities for this position include the development of infrastructure applications that improve the customer/user experience and the efficiency of the overall organization. Additionally, the application analyst provides guidance to internal teams in building models or tools to facilitate the gathering and reporting of metrics. The application analyst is responsible for identifying and exploring potential data sources and developing techniques to mine data. Lastly, the application analyst develops applications that provide the ability to track and search metadata to obtain results quickly.

The program coordinator and data specialist contributes to the consolidation and analysis of data at a detailed level. The project coordinator monitors project milestones and performs selected well-established, routine jobs for project team members. The coordinator also verifies project team members' work before it is released to the community. This verification process keeps work flowing and accurate, communications timely, and website information and measurements as up-to-date as possible. Major responsibilities for this position are to document and train library staff on new systems, processes, and procedures developed by the PMC, as well as to update, cleanse, and maintain metrics established by the analysts. The project coordinator documents current and proposed workflow diagrams, identifying problem areas, duplication, inefficiencies, and areas for improvements. In the project management arena, the coordinator also monitors and collects data on project teams, tracking the status of team progress for the library administration.

The director provides project management leadership to the library's senior management team, as team members familiarize themselves with the operating concepts of the PMC. The director also develops partnerships with organizations outside of the library such as Information Technology, the Office of Institutional Research and Assessment, business leadership, and other key stakeholders to define opportunities and to identify and prioritize common projects. The director's major responsibilities are to define and develop enterprise-wide program/project management practices, governance standards, processes, and metrics. The director also provides strategic leadership for the PMC, facilitates the development and implementation of projects, sustains a culture of continuous process improvement methodology, and ensures consistency in the team deliverables. The director acts as a key resource to senior leaders for analytical support in cross-functional areas. This relationship fosters development of an analytical culture among internal process owners and vendor partners.

The director reports to the dean of libraries and is a member of the library's senior management team. The director attends a weekly meeting with the associate deans and directors, as a member of the Dean's Team. This relationship helps the Dean's Team to understand the PMC charter and how assessment, metrics, and quality standards support the library's goals.

Reporting to the dean also levels the playing field for the director of PMC with the directors of other university functions, making it easier to conduct joint ventures and projects requiring assistance from outside the library. The job of the director is as much to facilitate with organizations and departments outside of the library as it is within the library. For example, the director works with the School of Information Studies and the Office of Institutional Research and Assessment on joint metric projects, as well as the campus Information Technology Department.

Gate and Security Alarm Project

Syracuse University's library administration regards an accurate under-standing of patron usage of library facilities as critical for demonstrating the library's value to the university and facilitating information-based decision making. This information is used in many ways, to scale library resources and staff or to determine space requirements. Information about patrons and their demographics, in particular, impacts most aspects of library operations. This impact makes knowledge of our patrons and their needs a critical component for the library to provide effective service.

While there are many library metrics, the Gate Count and Security Alarm Project illustrates the process that the PMC typically uses when reviewing and improving a method or procedure. The project focused on the count of people who go through the entrance/exit gates at Bird Library and instances of security alarm activation.

The security gates at each entrance/exit point at Syracuse University's Bird Library count each time a person passes through an entrance or exit. An alarm is sounded when an incorrectly checked out library item passes through the gate. Bird Library staff did not have an established process to follow when a security gate was not recording properly, resulting in an inability to accurately record the number of individuals passing through an entrance/exit that day. This lack of consistency led to a misrepresentation of the library's usage. The PMC decided to review the gate count metric as one of its first projects because the data was critical to library and university administration.

In analyzing the gate process, the Six Sigma five-step approach was used: Define, Measure, Analyze, Improve and Control. The first step was to thor-oughly define the problem and document the current process through inter-viewing personnel, and then creating a flow chart that represented the actual current process. (See figure 4.1.)

After stakeholders concurred on the current process flow, it was analyzed for inefficiencies, extraneous tasks, and areas for improvement. Four areas for improvement were identified: inconsistency in data collection and calcula-tion, inaccuracy in gate counts, inefficient collection practices, and infrequent

FIGURE 4.1

Current Flow for Recording Gate Count Data

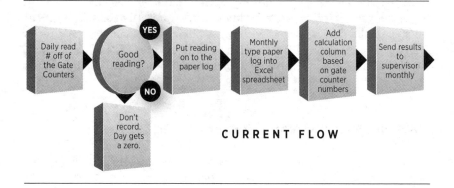

FIGURE 4.2

Current Flow for Recording Gate Count Data with Brainstorming Comments

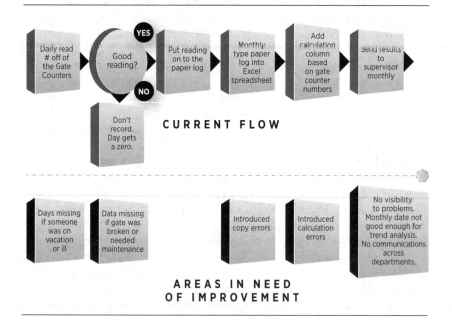

reporting. The team brainstormed and researched better ways to accomplish the same goal with fewer resources. (See figure 4.2.)

The inconsistency in data collection and calculation was caused by multiple people gathering and recording the data and using an inconsistent methodology. Gate counts at both entrance/exit points were gathered manually on paper and then later transferred to a monthly spreadsheet. This process was both antiquated in practice and inefficient. The issue of inconsistency in data collection was resolved by assigning a single person the responsibility to capture the data daily using a set protocol for documentation and calculation. A web form was created by the PMC application analyst to facilitate the daily entry of gate data from any computer workstation. The form automatically calculates the gate count, increasing accuracy and efficiency. It also works with Microsoft's SharePoint software to populate web-accessible graphs, or dashboards, updated in real time. These dashboards, created from the daily gate count input, have fostered better communication by making the collected data accessible to the rest of the organization.

The web form has also addressed the infrequent reporting issue identified during the initial process analysis. Prior gate count report compilations were made monthly in a way that did not permit analysis of trends. A report comparing the same month for several years proved to be more enlightening than one comparing data daily for one month. Standardized, valid reports can now be created and analyzed using the SharePoint software. This has facilitated easy access to data for trend analysis.

Before the changes that were identified through the analysis and brainstorming sessions were implemented, however, a proposed future flow was created. This flow would be used to ensure that there was nothing missing and that the new processes did not introduce any new errors. It also served as a document that all could review, understand, and sign off on as approval to move forward. (See figure 4.3.)

The suggested modifications were incorporated in the proposed flow, which graphically showed how automation and the workflow changes would improve the process. Once understood and approved by the team and stakeholders, changes were incorporated into the new procedure. The responsible individual was retrained to capture and input the data daily. With the standardization of the data collection and the automation of the process, daily trend analysis graphs were produced which revealed that there was a steady increase in building usage. After implementation, the new gate count was made visible to the entire library staff through the SharePoint dashboard. This dashboard is monitored by the PMC and if an outlier is found, an investigation is launched to determine the cause of the outlying data point. Inaccuracies in typed numbers and computer glitches are caught quickly by the dashboard monitoring process and are addressed before measurements are effected.

FIGURE 4.3

Proposed Future Flow for Recording Gate Count Data

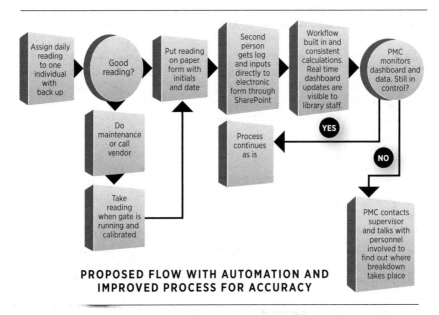

PROPOSED FLOW WITH AUTOMATION AND
IMPROVED PROCESS FOR ACCURACY

A by-product and real benefit that came from the Gate Count Project was the discovery of the capability to capture the number of times the gate security alarms were activated. This was an issue because every time the alarm activates, a library staff member has to retrieve the person who activated the alarm and determine why the alarm activated. Further, faculty believed the library had a theft problem. Thus, investigating the reason for the alarm activations was added to the Gate Count Project's scope. While identifying the cause of each gate alarm activation was manual and more difficult to determine, this identification process was critical since an alarm meant the potential loss of library materials.

Initially fifteen different reasons for the alarm activation were identified. We combined similar reasons and came up with six basic categories for which solutions were found and implemented. A Pareto graph was created, demonstrating that only a small percentage of alarm activations were due to an actual failure to check out library materials, intentional theft, or patron forgetfulness. (See figure 4.4.)

Two main reasons for alarm activation were improper desensitization of books at both staffed and self-check circulation stations. This problem was addressed by asking the vendor of the self-check machines to recalibrate this

FIGURE 4.4

Pareto Chart of Reasons for Gate Alarm Activations

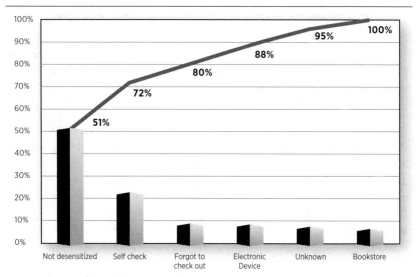

ALARMS BEFORE SOLUTIONS

equipment and by retraining staff at the circulation desk. Electronic devices, including cell phones, also activated the alarms. To prevent electronics from triggering the alarms, 3M, the security gate manufacturer, was asked to recalibrate the security gates. Staff then learned how to clean the gates weekly to maintain the machinery and avoid further glitches. Other causes of alarm activation included outside sources such as the bookstore. Recalibration of the gates and preventative maintenance also reduced the number of activations from bookstore books. After these changes were implemented, the PMC continually monitored alarm activation metrics to ensure that the changes did not introduce any new errors. After five months, activation of security alarms was reduced by 75 percent.

The Gate Count and Security Alarm Project demonstrated that the library did not have a theft problem, as some faculty members believed, but the security alarm issue was more complex. Once the issues were addressed, the alarms, while still heard, were heard less frequently. By addressing the Gate Count data collection issues, the library was able to show the university administration that the library was busier than it had ever been, with an increase from 876,464 people in 2009 to 1,017,148 in 2010—a 16 percent increase in a single year. With the new data documenting the increase in usage, we were able to justify additional support from the maintenance department for custodial help, which we had not been able to do in the past.

The combination of more efficient and consistent data collection with real increases in resource availability has proven to be a powerful staff motivator. It was very important for the people collecting the data and responsible for managing the processes to know how this data was being used. If they do not understand the value of the data, they may lose interest in collecting it properly and thoroughly. It is the PMC's responsibility to ensure that everyone involved sees how the Gate Count data is being used and understands not only how it affects their function, but other functions within the library as well. This understanding is motivational and also provides the staff with knowledge of how the various functions of the library work together. This increased understanding improves internal communications, as well as service to the patron.

The Gate Count dashboards have served as a powerful tool for demonstrating to the university administration the increased usage of the library facilities, resulting in real benefits to the library, such as improved custodial services. The dean of libraries now has more data at her disposal when advocating for budgets for facilities and services. Recent budget requests were granted because the library could demonstrate that there were significantly more visitors. Additional services were required to keep the patrons happy and the library appropriately cleaned and staffed.

Library Measures Data Repository

Although the dashboards are the most visible data initiative supported by the PMC, they represent a small portion of the more comprehensive collection of qualitative and quantitative data reports made available to staff via its Library Measures data repository. The repository arose from the need for a centralized, more accessible, and more sophisticated approach to the use of data at the library. A data audit conducted in 2007 revealed that most data collected within departments was used to evaluate local operations, and was stored on local shared drives available only to staff within that department. The PMC's task was to identify departmental data, document how it was gathered, create efficiencies for its collection, and consolidate data for improved trend analysis.

The planning of the repository consisted of several steps. The first was to identify the potential scope of its contents. The Library Measures repository serves the entire library and contains files of both quantitative and qualitative data from all functional areas of the library. While routine reports tend to be numbers-based, the repository also contains textual data such as student feedback comments from surveys, usability test reports, and summaries of qualitative interviews. In planning for access workflows, the PMC team considered who the users of the repository would be and how they would interact with the files. This led to the key questions of determining levels of security, permissions for adding content to the site, and provisions for oversight of the repository's content, its accuracy and currency. The ideal repository would provide access to data for multiple audiences: from raw data for use by PMC staff for generating customized reports, to slide presentations with charts and graphs available for the library administration to use with external stakeholders.

Determining scope and user access led to questions of metadata, that is, how files would be described in systematic ways for optimal searching and retrieval. SharePoint supports multiple systems for describing content in the repository. The PMC used this functionality to develop structured metadata with specific terminology to describe methodology, functional service areas, date coverage, and key data fields included in the file. In addition, SharePoint allows for open-ended textual file descriptions, tagging, and "favorites" so that users can more easily identify and access the data they use most often.

In a setting where library staff is accustomed to using local shared drives for access to data and collaborative work, placing secure documents "on the Web" seemed to be an insecure solution. Staff buy-in for the repository was needed so that it would be perceived as a safe place to store important data. The technical requirements for the repository tool included tight permissions control, as well as version control to adequately support sharing of documents and collaboration. The SharePoint product met these requirements for accessibility, including file versioning, permissions controls based on the university's active directory, and web-based functional support for creating workflow efficiencies.

The PMC took responsibility for the organizational structure and repository workflows, developing standards for documentation, naming conventions, and training staff in the use of the repository. While the data repository represents a new approach to organizing data and making it more visible, the true test of its value is its use throughout the organization. An ongoing and multipronged training program is an important component of ensuring that data is being used and understood properly. Training includes one-on-one sessions, online tools, and staff presentations. An online instruction guide was created to introduce the Library Measures repository, its organization, and provide links to key data files and dashboards. This guide (http://research guides.library.syr.edu/librarymeasures/) was used to walk staff through the site as it was presented at department meetings. These sessions allowed for the gathering of feedback from staff that was then incorporated into the tool. The success of the repository will be monitored via use statistics as well as the social tools that SharePoint provides users for tagging and liking files.

As the use of the Library Measures repository grows, expectations for data availability are shifting. With the move from operational monthly data to long-term trend data and from single institutional data to comparative data, library staff ask questions that are more complex, such as what journal titles are requested most frequently through interlibrary loan and by whom or how the rate of circulation varies throughout the collection based on Library of Congress classification and date of acquisition.

The centralized approach taken by the PMC to data collection allows for the correlation of library data with institutional demographic data. For the first time questions such as what departments are using which electronic databases and how circulation of library books and user status are interrelated can be addressed. Additionally, the centralization has resulted in the ability to conduct trend analyses and to compare Syracuse data with that of peer institutions.

Conclusion

The Program Management Center continues to evolve. As projects are successfully completed, there are more requests for data and more demand for the PMC to manage or coordinate new projects.

Further, with the centralization of data and the expertise for its collection and analysis in the PMC, library managers are asking more complex and difficult questions. We strive for a balance between providing distilled data for external customers and developing dashboards and other easy-to-use systems that allow staff to use data independently. Our tools and reports must address a wide range of audiences and stakeholders—from library managers and staff to university administrators. Customizing data reports to the appropriate audience level requires careful attention.

The importance of training cannot be overestimated. While changing processes can be difficult, providing easily available, timely, and continuous training can often make the difference in the successful implementation of new, more efficient procedures. We worry that data provided in its raw form will be misinterpreted when taken out of context. We also recognize the reality of university decision making. Money, emotions, and politics, as well as data, must be considered. Not all decisions can be entirely driven by data.

The PMC approach has realized benefits related to staff motivation, problem solving, and developing a culture of assessment at the library. We've learned that metrics can be motivational for staff. The Gate Count Project illustrated how metrics can become a motivator when the staff members gathering data witnessed that positive facility changes resulted from the information they collected.

Making data more visible also leads to discussion of trends and, in turn, discussion of solutions for new approaches, new procedures, and new services. As an example, while we see an increasing trend in the use of our building as a study facility, we see a decrease in the use of our traditional reference desk. Those facts motivate us to think about using more social media to conduct reference and roving through the building, rather than sitting at a service desk.

Finally, while we recognize that the measures we use to evaluate quality and value for the library are constantly evolving, the approach to standardizing these measures and analyzing them will remain a necessary part of library assessment. The PMC has contributed to an increased awareness of data and its importance for library planning and growth.

NOTE

1. Kai Yang and Basem S. El-Hai, *Design for Six Sigma* (New York: McGraw-Hill Professional, 2008).

BARBARA P. SILCOX, MARY-
DEIRDRE CORAGGIO, SUSAN
MAKAR, AND MYLENE OUIMETTE

Information Services Office, National
Institute of Standards and Technology

5
Thriving through Organizational Agility

The NIST Information Services
Office's Baldrige Journey

ORGANIZATIONAL AGILITY IS THE CAPACITY TO QUICKLY IDEN-
tify and capitalize on opportunities to successfully meet and exceed customer expectations. This capability, critical to an organization's success, can
be achieved and sustained using evidenced-based assessment practices and
by managing an organization from a holistic point of view. The Baldrige Criteria for Performance Excellence are used by thousands of U.S. organizations
to provide this holistic view for measuring and improving performance.[1] The
Information Services Office (ISO) at the National Institute of Standards and
Technology (NIST) began its Baldrige journey in 1997; ten years later it was
awarded the Maryland Silver Quality Award by the Maryland Performance
Excellence Award program.

This chapter addresses how the ISO uses the Baldrige Framework to guide
and propel our organization forward. It explains why this view of organizational management works so well for us and how it can be implemented by
other libraries. It describes how the systematic management and assessment
approaches taken by the ISO strengthened our organization's ability to respond
quickly to rapidly changing technologies and rising customer expectations.

The chapter discusses how the ISO introduces new hires into its organizational culture. It shows how the ISO involves the entire workforce in all aspects of strategic and operational planning and organizational assessment to build a depth of commitment to excellence and leadership. It presents specific examples of approaches and systems, identified as "role model" practices, which can be adapted and used by other library organizations. These role model practices include (1) the ISO's Lab Liaison Program, which serves as a key mechanism for listening to and partnering with our customers; (2) the Vision Implementation Project, which helps to promote understanding and staff involvement in vision implementation; and (3) the ISO's Workforce Development and Performance Management Systems, which define how employee work assignments are aligned with professional development and the organizations' strategic and operational plans. The chapter concludes with some considerations for the organization's future directions and how it may continue to flourish in a tight budget climate.

Background

The ISO is an award-winning organization with a deeply rooted commitment to customer service excellence and a culture that encourages risk taking, learning, and assessment.[2] This commitment and culture are woven through the organization's mission and values, which are reviewed, reaffirmed, or updated by the entire organization on a yearly basis. The ISO's mission is "to support and enhance NIST's scientific and technological community through a comprehensive program of knowledge management." To support this mission, the ISO provides professional scientific and technical information assistance to NIST research staff throughout their research and publishing cycles through the activities of three programs: the Research Library and Information Program, the Electronic Information and Publications Program, and the Museum and History Program.

The ISO accomplishes its mission with a workforce of twenty-eight, which includes the office director and the two program managers, all of whom are professional librarians. The Research Library Information Program consists of six professional librarians, six support staff, and a business specialist. The Electronic Information and Publications Program consists of four professional librarians, two technical information specialists, a program analyst, a writer/editor, and three support staff. No staff are specifically assigned to the Museum and History Program. A secretary, who reports to the office director, rounds out the workforce.

While employees are officially assigned to a specific program and supervisor, they typically work across organizational lines. This enables the organization to target the most appropriate talent and expertise to any given project, and effectively manage workload according to priorities. The program managers have direct line supervision and share responsibilities for providing input to and reviewing the work that crosses programs. This approach to operating and managing the organization is driven by the Knowledge Continuum, a concept first introduced in 1993 by the former library director. The concept is based on the premise that the processes that contribute to the creation of new knowledge in the research environment form part of a continuum which has no beginning or end. Therefore, research institutions are best served by library organizations that extend their role in the scholarly research process beyond supporting research discovery, to producing and disseminating research results. In implementing the concept within the ISO, "management sought to capitalize on, and extend an organizational structure that was formally in place as a single unit, but was in reality working as a composite of distinct and unrelated units."[3] While many libraries in academic institutions have been providing some form of publishing services since 2007, the approach adopted by the ISO was novel when first introduced in 1993.[4]

Through a concerted effort by management, the Knowledge Continuum has provided the overarching philosophy that drives how the ISO operates as one cohesive organization. The ISO's products and services are mapped to the Continuum and it forms the framework for defining organizational and workforce competencies. New employees are introduced to the Knowledge Continuum concept early via the ISO employee handbook. The Continuum concept and how it translates into services and design of work systems is also reinforced regularly at staff meetings.

By respecting our organization's stated values and the overarching philosophy of the Knowledge Continuum, the ISO workforce exemplifies the commitment to excellence that enables our organization to go beyond customer expectations. The Baldrige Framework provides the means for sustaining this commitment to excellence. Together, the Knowledge Continuum and the Baldrige Framework underpin the ISO's approach to management and assessment to ensure that the organization remains agile and stays focused on results, impacts, and creating value for stakeholders and customers.

The Baldrige Criteria and Framework

The Baldrige Criteria for Performance Excellence is an assessment tool which any organization can use to evaluate and improve its overall performance.[5] The criteria consist of sets of questions within seven key categories deemed critical to successful organizational performance. These categories form a framework for managing an organization. The questions posed in each category of the criteria serve as the guide for examining how well the organization operates. The Baldrige Criteria do not prescribe specific management practices or methods; organizations must devise and document practices and methods that are most suitable for their environment. The criteria do provide a structured, holistic approach for determining effective operations and performance. Six categories—leadership; strategic planning; customer focus; measurement, analysis, and knowledge management; workforce focus; and operations focus—work together and form the basis for setting strategy and improvement targets, as well as analyzing results to determine overall organizational performance.

We are often asked why a library should struggle with such a complex method for managing and assessing an organization. There are several reasons. Our first answer applies to any organization choosing to use the criteria. You can start small and build on your successes. There is nothing in the criteria that requires you to tackle all of the criteria categories at once. As long as you keep the entire framework in mind, you can begin by choosing one category or elements of several categories. The ISO began with strategic planning (Category 2), addressing skills mix issues (Category 5), and learning more about our customers (Category 3). All efforts were, and continue to be, focused on the entire Baldrige Framework and the Knowledge Continuum.

While the Baldrige Criteria and Framework appear to be complex, they can be adapted to any size or type of organization. The criteria and framework merely provide the parameters and the lens through which an organization can design and assess its management approaches. How those approaches are implemented directly determines the results. Nothing in the Baldrige Criteria specifies the right answers for ensuring that you formulate the shrewdest strategic plans, create the most efficient work processes, or select the most appropriate and valid measurements.

Our second answer applies specifically to libraries. To say that libraries are both customer- and process-oriented trivializes what every professional librarian learns during their graduate studies and the roles most research libraries play in their organizations. Libraries are large, complex information systems. Librarians, by training, take a systems-oriented approach to solving problems for their customers. The Baldrige Framework is a systems approach to organizational management that overlays well with the principles of information systems management. The theory and principles of information systems influence the way librarians think and act. For example, helping library customers with their information needs is often a process of joint problem analysis and problem solving. This process starts with asking questions, identifying and anticipating customers' needs, determining priorities, and balancing trade-offs to find the best solution. The process is often cyclical and involves obtaining feedback from the customer and evaluating the approaches used to determine that the actions taken were appropriate and had the desired outcome and impact. It is this systems-oriented thinking that librarians acquire through education or develop through experience that enables them to apply the approaches outlined in the Baldrige Criteria.

The Baldrige Criteria provide the approaches we use to understand and manage organizational and individual performance. They guide the way we think and act strategically; they help us ask questions about how we conduct business; and they help us focus on results and impacts. Following the criteria, the ISO links strategic and operational goals with customer requirements, key processes, and workforce development to achieve success. Employee performance plans and individual development plans are directly linked to the ISO's strategic and operational plans. This alignment and connectivity, as well as a focus on assessment and continuous improvement, enable the ISO to respond quickly to changing technologies and customer expectations and requirements. (See figure 5.1.) Further, our knowledge and understanding of our customers gained through regular and ongoing assessment activities contribute greatly to our agility. The keys to our success are simple—we listen, learn, assess, partner, and collaborate. We are comfortable with critically evaluating our triumphs and failures. We recognize our success results from leadership, celebrating successes—both large and small—and focusing on results and impact.

While the ISO adopted the Baldrige Framework for managing our organization, we do not undertake its use with an unrealistic adherence to every item listed in each of the criteria categories. Nor do we find ourselves unduly entangled in defining and capturing every process and improvement strategy. As a small organization, there is an important balance between documenting and measuring every process and making decisions based on a priori knowledge to keep moving forward. We focus on the big picture and rely on our professional training and experience to ground us. We also continue to instill in our workforce a strong regard for creativity, trying new things, taking calculated risks, being responsive to the customer, and learning from both successes and mistakes. This sometimes requires a leap of faith rather than strict conformance with any particular decision-making process or management tool.

There are valuable principles within the Baldrige Criteria and Framework that have assisted the ISO in improving and sustaining its overall performance. These principles include visionary leadership, organizational learning, customer-driven performance, a cross-trained and engaged workforce, and a focus on results. We continue to build and maintain credibility with our customers and stakeholders by implementing evidenced-based practices. We are keenly aware of and can take advantage of our strengths and are able to identify and correct our weaknesses. Most important, we have developed an organization that is quick-thinking, effectively manages its resources, uses data to make decisions, and continues to build a loyal customer base.

FIGURE 5.1

ISO Activities Mapped to the Baldrige Framework

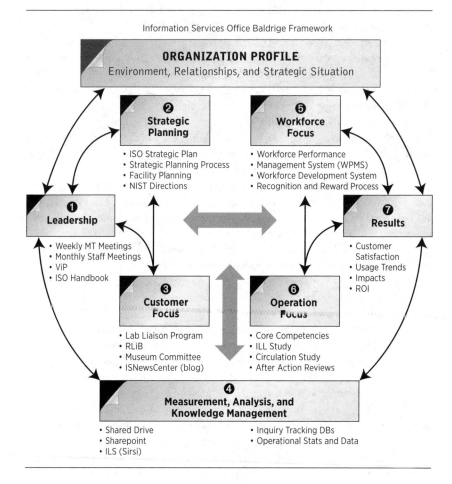

Information Services Office Baldrige Framework

ORGANIZATION PROFILE
Environment, Relationships, and Strategic Situation

❷ **Strategic Planning**

• ISO Strategic Plan
• Strategic Planning Process
• Facility Planning
• NIST Directions

❺ **Workforce Focus**

• Workforce Performance
• Management System (WPMS)
• Workforce Development System
• Recognition and Reward Process

❶ **Leadership**

• Weekly MT Meetings
• Monthly Staff Meetings
• ViP
• ISO Handbook

❼ **Results**

• Customer Satisfaction
• Usage Trends
• Impacts
• ROI

❸ **Customer Focus**

• Lab Liaison Program
• RLiB
• Museum Committee
• ISNewsCenter (blog)

❻ **Operation Focus**

• Core Competencies
• ILL Study
• Circulation Study
• After Action Reviews

❹ **Measurement, Analysis, and Knowledge Management**

• Shared Drive
• Sharepoint
• ILS (Sirsi)

• Inquiry Tracking DBs
• Operational Stats and Data

Building a Culture Focused on Knowledge Sharing, Improvement, and Results

Since the early 1990s, the ISO leadership has taken significant steps to create and reinforce an environment that fosters knowledge sharing and agility, stimulates innovative thinking, and ensures organizational sustainability. The Baldrige Criteria recognize the importance of leaders' actions in establishing this environment. Efforts to develop a quick-thinking, managerially effective organization with a loyal customer base began long before the Baldrige

FIGURE 5.2

ISO Mission, Vision, and Values

Mission

To support and enhance NIST's scientific and technological community through a comprehensive program of knowledge management

Vision

To be globally recognized as the premier science and technology information resource for measurement science

Values

- To be a trusted provider of information products and services through a knowledgeable, responsive, and professional staff
- To anticipate and exceed our customers' expectations
- To be always accessible to and approachable by our customers
- To create an atmosphere within ISO that inspires superior performance by all its employees
- To develop new services and products through open communication and by encouraging risk taking
- To strive to obtain new resources and make the most efficient use of existing resources
- To develop and use teamwork based on trust, mutual respect, and pride

Framework became part of our culture. These efforts, however, were critical in setting the course for our adoption of the Baldrige approaches to performance excellence. We attribute the ISO's ongoing agility to the ongoing actions taken by the ISO leadership; our close connection to our customer; our understanding of our internal processes and the effect they have on our customers; our focus on improvement and staying ahead of customer requirements; our mechanisms for sharing knowledge with our customers and with one another; and our focus on results and impact.

Following the introduction of the Knowledge Continuum, the ISO created a vision, mission, and set of values. (See figure 5.2.) These statements have largely withstood the test of time, undergoing a few slight revisions since their creation in 1997. Our values underpin our organization's emphasis on knowledge sharing, customer-driven excellence, risk taking, and teamwork, while our mission and vision serve as the context for our strategic and operational plans.

Identity plays a large role in living our values and pursuing our vision. The ISO workforce has developed a strong, team-oriented, customer-centric identity. Staff are confident they are listening to customers and responding with well-defined expertise. They are sure of and proud of the ISO's well-branded products. This confidence and pride is evidenced in their interactions with customers and articulated in the many formal discussions and informal conversations ISO leaders have with customers and staff. Knowledge sharing; frank, open communication on issues affecting the organization; and communication of long- and short-term strategic and operational plans occur at monthly ISO staff meetings. This inspires trust between all levels of the organization and serves as a tool for preventing and eliminating communication barriers. Our open communication is a result of continuous and persistent efforts made by ISO leaders.

Identity and values also play important roles in our hiring process, influencing what we look for in candidates, and how we handle interviews and selection. While credentials are important, the ISO pays particular attention to qualified candidates who best fit our organization. Staff are integral members of the interviewing team, reporting their assessment of candidates to the hiring official. Newly hired employees are paired with a buddy who, along with the supervisor, orients the employee to the ISO and the larger institution. All employees are given an ISO employee handbook. This document addresses topics specific to the ISO's management approaches and culture, such as the Knowledge Continuum; strategic plans and the planning process; knowledge sharing; and our implementation of Baldrige.

Knowledge sharing is a key element that binds our organizational culture. Monthly program-level meetings, in addition to our monthly staff meetings, allow staff the opportunity to delve into project details and receive suggestions and input from staff not involved in a project. Processes and workflow are refined during these meetings and staff share what they are hearing from their customers. Since agility requires trust and action to accomplish organizational objectives and this trust is gained through listening and sharing, there are no secrets. All staff are encouraged to share their ideas and concerns about all projects. From our staff and program-level meetings, new hires quickly learn about the work conducted throughout the organization and the importance of sharing and learning from one another.

If knowledge sharing unites the ISO internally, it also inspires trust and confidence externally with our customers. The ISO uses many mechanisms for building customer relationships. While seminars, open houses, and training sessions to demonstrate research tools and informatics methods are part of our repertoire, proactive two-way communication undertaken with individual customers is most effective. Even our most loyal customers continue to be amazed at what we can do for them.

Agility also requires consistent attention to operational and strategic plans. The ISO takes a rigorous and systematic approach to planning, recognizing that planning heightens staff awareness of organizational directions, customer expectations, and stakeholder requirements. The ISO welcomes and encourages "out of the box" thinking and incorporates it into organizational structures and planning processes. Innovation and creativity thrive in the ISO because the playground is surrounded by processes and systems that create an infrastructure capable of sustaining a complex organization equipped to quickly adopt new ideas. The role model practices described later in this chapter are examples of the processes and systems that provide fertile ground for identifying and implementing internal improvements. Improvements are made by starting small, but keeping the big picture in mind.

Tracking and monitoring results is vital to achieving organizational agility. Knowing what data to collect, how frequently to collect it, and how to interpret it is critical to sustaining performance excellence. The Baldrige Criteria call for organizations to "select and use data and information for performance measurement, analysis, and review in support of organizational planning and performance improvement."[6] The ISO regularly conducts assessment activities to gain an understanding of its performance. These activities are integrated into all phases of planning and service delivery. These activities are also embedded in employee annual performance plans. Staff routinely conduct after-action reviews at the conclusion of most projects, whether large or small, and employee performance plans typically include the language "ensures ISO projects are assessed for impact; works with other ISO staff to ensure data is collected, analyzed, and synthesized for decision-making and repurposing to stakeholders and customers." Results require examining performance and outcomes critically and independently against benchmarks and standards, in relation to competitors, and against customer requirements. Over the years, the ISO's assessment initiatives have included large customer satisfaction surveys, benchmark studies, focus groups, customer requirement and use studies, and workforce satisfaction studies.[7] In addition to these large assessment activities, ISO routinely collects and analyzes transactional usage and satisfaction data to understand and anticipate customer and stakeholder requirements.

Reviewing and examining our processes and services in relation to data on performance, transactional requirements, and customer satisfaction lead to incremental improvements. Examining and taking actions on workforce feedback, for example, improve staff responsiveness, loyalty, and leadership. The ISO lives in a state of constant change that can be both challenging and disruptive. However, our ability to successfully adapt to change reflects on the ISO's flexible and agile nature. This is a direct result of our culture, vision, and values as well as our systematic approach to managing the organization and assessing its health.

Role Model Practices

Our role model practices are the direct results of leadership, planning, strong processes, knowledge sharing, and assessment. All are connected to one another through the lens of the Baldrige Framework and Criteria, which state that "a sustainable organization is capable of addressing current business needs and possesses the agility and strategic management to prepare successfully for its future business, market, and operating environments."[8] The ISO's Lab Liaison Program and Vision Implementation Project (ViP) are examples of actions taken by the ISO's leadership to create a sustainable, agile organization. The ISO's Workforce Development and Performance Management Systems are examples of the ISO's mechanisms for supporting high-performance work. While some role model practices are born of innovation and take hold more quickly, others are the result of implementing cohesive processes. Each of the following role model practices falls into one of these categories.

ISO's Lab Liaison Program

In 1997 ISO leaders realized that for the ISO to achieve its vision, it needed a more collaborative relationship with customers. To build relationships with key customers specifically, they initially created a Research Consultants Program, which evolved into the Lab Liaison Program in 2002. Today lab liaisons partner and collaborate with NIST scientists and other technical staff on a variety of strategic research activities. Liaisons are assigned to NIST labs and programs to establish and maintain close working relationships with managers and scientists within these organizations. They serve as personal consultants to researchers in each lab or program, contributing their expertise to lab research and planning activities, and are the researchers' primary point of contact with the ISO. Liaisons work directly with NIST researchers to help assess the impact of researchers' work and to identify the best places for researchers to publish to reach their intended audience. Liaisons gather and analyze market and industry data, and educate labs and programs about the advantages of using the ISO's resources and customized services. They also gather feedback for ISO strategic planning, enhancing products and services, and improving operational processes.

Lab liaisons use a variety of mechanisms for establishing and maintaining relationships with customers. These include attending and presenting at lab meetings, meeting one-on-one with bench scientists and lab management, addressing new employees at NIST New Employee Orientation sessions, attending and contributing to lab events and special activities, and participating in NIST-wide committees. Liaisons stay abreast of their lab's research and programmatic activities through their relationships with customers by monitoring the *NIST Monthly Highlights* and by hosting the monthly Research Library Board meetings.

Since 1997, the Lab Liaison Program concept has been a major component of the ISO's strategic plan, and the importance of the program to the ISO's strategic success remains constant. Today the Lab Liaison Program is at the forefront in furthering the ISO's strategic goals "to help advance and position NIST research and publishing activities for maximum impacts" and "to increase the visibility and use of ISO services and resources."

Lab liaisons play a critical role in collecting and analyzing data for performance assessment and improvement. They use many mechanisms to gather information about customers, and as a result are able to suggest analyses or develop information products in advance of customers' requests. Liaisons have conducted many highly visible projects on behalf of or in collaboration with their customers, such as analyzing publishing impacts for an entire NIST lab; formulating publishing strategies to help labs achieve maximum impact; conducting comprehensive literature reviews that became part of researchers' papers; developing methods for researchers to share sources for hard-to-find scientific properties data; measuring relative impact against peer research institutions; and examining the state of scientific or technical research at U.S. universities to assess U.S. competitiveness in the global marketplace.

At the completion of each project, liaisons seek feedback from the customer. This feedback is used to refine research analysis methods and to extend or plan additional products or services for new groups. Liaisons record this feedback and other information about their projects and collaborations using a central tracking tool. This data is reviewed regularly by the liaisons and ISO leaders for the purposes of planning, refining, or creating new products and services.

A key component of the Liaison Program is collaboration among the liaisons. Liaisons share information, strategies, and accomplishments at biweekly meetings, which offer a forum for reviewing customer requests and feedback, and for developing and critiquing potential strategies for meeting customer needs. These meetings are also used as training sessions to learn about new analysis tools, methods, and resources. Discussions often result in liaisons working together to develop action plans or methods for meeting customer needs. For large, extensive projects, liaisons make recommendations to ISO leadership on the methods and skills needed to meet the project requirements, as well as budgetary considerations. They also provide a time line for carrying out the project.

Each liaison has an individual, self-created strategy plan that maps out tailored approaches for communicating, educating, and working with their assigned lab or program. While individual plans may differ in the methods and strategies used to meet the Liaison Program goals, the goals of collaboration and outreach are the same.

ISO leadership supports the Lab Liaison Program by emphasizing the skills, expertise, and values required for success. This support is reflected in their recruitment for new hires and through their budgeting for training and professional development. The ISO seeks individuals who are excellent communicators with strong customer service abilities and values. Writing skills are essential since liaisons create reports and write detailed analyses for their customers. Liaisons typically have backgrounds in scientific or technical areas and substantial experience and expertise in information research and analysis. While professional development is a must for all ISO employees, liaisons are particularly encouraged and active in organizations such as the Special Libraries Association, the Society for Scholarly Publishing, and the National Information Standards Organization.

The Liaison Program provides an illustrative example of ISO workforce engagement to achieve high performance. ISO leaders encourage each liaison to formulate their own recommendations for how to best interact with their assigned lab and to develop appropriate work products or services. Though this is an inherent risk, each liaison is able to work creatively and independently to establish collaborative relationships within their respective lab. Each liaison also understands the importance of collaborating and sharing knowledge with other liaisons. It is this knowledge sharing that makes the Liaison Program a success.

Vision Implementation Project

In 2005 the ISO director created the Vision Implementation Project (ViP) to promote staff understanding of and involvement in vision implementation, to position staff to act as change agents by boosting staff-to-staff influence, and to help staff understand connections between operational plans, strategic goals, and the organization's vision. The ViP is comprised of three ISO staff members with varying professional or educational backgrounds and with various functional roles within the organization. The ViP's goals are to develop ideas that facilitate the translation of the ISO's vision into actual operations. The ViP's projects, activities, and products help the ISO navigate the pathways between strategic and operational goals and also help the organization identify means for increasing its visibility within the NIST.

Fundamentally, the ViP serves as a think tank, helping the ISO to stay abreast of future trends and to remain attuned to the NIST's evolving vision for itself. ViP team members communicate with ISO staff in a variety of ways, encouraging ISO staff to share ideas with each other and contribute to envisioning the future for the organization. The ViP recognizes that the changing information infrastructure creates many new challenges, threats, and opportunities for the ISO. Future customers will have higher expectations for information services as a result of their technology fluency and preference for multitasking. Since its creation, the ViP has led the ISO staff in a variety of workshops on topics such as the information ecosystem and the ISO's web presence, customer workflow analysis, and research trends to address issues of strategic interest to the organization. Each workshop has allowed the staff to grapple with issues and emerging trends in the library and publishing industries and think about ways the ISO can meet current and future customer expectations.

The ViP documents its findings and presents results for each activity in the form of a written report for the ISO leadership and the staff. These results have influenced ISO activities and strategic directions by creating ongoing opportunities for the entire staff to participate in considering strategic issues of importance to the health and future of the organization. They also help staff think strategically and translate vision into reality.

ISO's Workforce Development and Performance Management Systems

The ISO's values support high-performance work, and engagement. (See figure 5.3.) Through individual development opportunities, challenging and varying work assignments, and incorporating opportunities for innovation and experimentation, ISO's iterative Workforce Development and Performance Management Systems provide the framework for high performance in individual and organizational achievement.

Communication at all levels is vital to the system's success. The systems enable regular, formal feedback opportunities between employees and supervisors to discuss projects and accomplishments and review performance. In addition, ISO leaders collaborate and share with one another to ensure that they are well informed and up-to-date regarding the status of projects across functions and organizational lines. Leaders also communicate regularly with staff through a variety of forums regarding ISO objectives, progress, and performance. This helps to reinforce the sense of ISO "identity" that contributes to workforce engagement.

Staff members also have a multitude of avenues for contributing feedback regarding individual tasks and responsibilities throughout the entire life cycle of yearly performance plans. Staff members submit descriptions of their

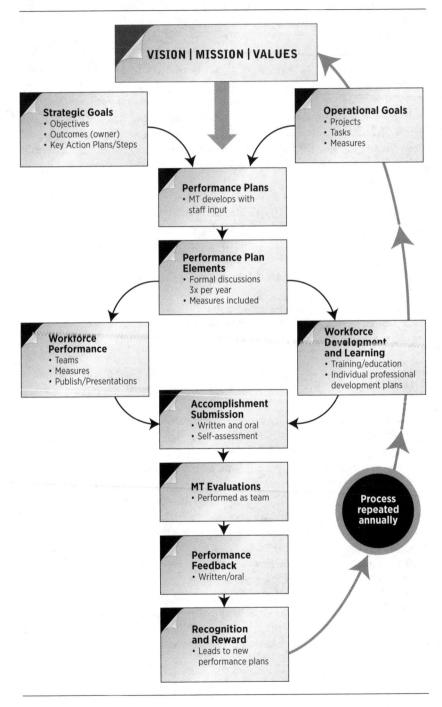

individual accomplishments to their direct supervisors using a standard template. This template provides a benchmark for comparison against the ISO's strategic and operational goals.

Individual development is a major priority and even in a tight budget climate, the ISO leadership supports professional development and training for all staff. The ISO began conducting intensive skills self-assessments in 2000, requiring staff members to rate their comfort and proficiency in a comprehensive range of skill areas. The results of this assessment form the basis for identifying skill set gaps and determining specific areas for improvement. Information on training opportunities inside and external to NIST and on potential venues for publishing and presenting is provided in the ISO Annual Professional Development Plan to guide the staff in creating their individual development plans (IDPs).

IDPs specify the employee's developmental short-term and long-term goals and include specific training or developmental opportunities for achieving those goals. Short-term goals must address the specific skill areas, work assignments, and success measures identified in the employee's annual performance plan. IDP requirements include training in areas of organizational development and leadership.

New knowledge and skills are reinforced on the job through knowledge-sharing activities and new work assignments. The ISO's emphasis on learning and sharing creates a contagious excitement that results in high levels of employee engagement and creativity. This emphasis on learning is also a critical ingredient for sustaining agility.

Conclusion

The ISO vision "to be globally recognized as the premier science and technology information resource for measurement science" remains clear. As we build on our successes, the keys to our future remain the same as our past—using a systematic approach to understanding and managing the organization.

Like other libraries, technological advances and developments in library and publishing standards lead to many of our initiatives. Not surprisingly, changes in key products and services require a stronger focus on management and delivery of digital content we both license or own. The Lab Liaison Program continues to aggressively pursue targeted strategic research activities. Liaisons' ongoing relationships with NIST researchers continue to thrive and grow. We are assessing the impact of our activities and services on the NIST community, to coincide with NIST's emphasis on measuring the impact of its research. This is no small challenge, but helps us to further demonstrate our value to the NIST.

A significant NIST realignment and reorganization initiated in fiscal year 2011 presents new challenges. Changes in customer demographics demand new approaches to library services. The economic downturn has affected resource allocation. Limited resources and long-term relevance and sustainability demand that the ISO focus on the right customers and identify areas where we have maximum impact. We recognize a need to exploit emerging publisher business models, such as pay-per-view, to enable discovery and access to content required by our customers. ISO teams are evaluating options to reengineer processes and more effectively use resources. Our quick response to this changing budgetary and publishing landscape is emblematic of our agility and commitment to performance excellence.

When using the Baldrige Criteria it is important to understand the meaning of "what" and "how." These differences are critical to assessing results and understanding if our approaches show evidence of deployment, learning, and alignment with organizational goals. Looking at the "how" allows us to view processes and service delivery in a way that permits diagnosis and feedback.

Like many organizations, we have struggled with selecting meaningful measures that give the best guidance for organizational planning and performance improvement. Transactional measures that give statistics on use, number of downloads, satisfaction, trends, and patterns, all tell a story and help us with decision making. Setting meaningful targets in an ever-changing environment and determining the best measures to assess impact are more complicated. In 2010, the ISO created a Measures Portfolio as a means for compiling information about what we have been measuring, how we capture the data, and determining what else we should be measuring. We intend to use this portfolio to select and build a system for integrating the right measures into our processes and planning.

We continue to evaluate our key processes, our improvements, and what we measure. Understanding the customer view of the value of our products and services leads to better performance. The ISO is eager to learn new assessment methods and to create vehicles to better manage our assessment information. We intend to focus on our internal collaboration processes, to streamline our data collection burden and improve our ease of sharing. Most important, translating our results into impact statements is critical to our future.

The Baldrige Framework is working for the ISO. It influences how we approach our immediate future to sustain our agile and viable program. We believe this framework lends itself well to libraries looking to shape their future.

NOTES

1. Baldrige Performance Excellence Program, *Criteria for Performance Excellence, 2011–2012* (Gaithersburg, MD: National Institute of Standards and Technology, 2011).

2. In 2003 and 2008 the organization received the Federal Library of the Year Award from the Federal Library and Information Center Committee in recognition of its innovative practices and customer focus.

3. Paul Vassallo, "The Knowledge Continuum—Organizing for Research and Scholarly Communication," *Internet Research: Electronic Networking Applications and Policy* 9, no. 3 (1999): 232–42.

4. Karla L. Hahn, *Research Library Publishing Services: New Options for University Publishing* (Washington, DC: Association of Research Libraries, 2008).

5. The Baldrige Criteria for Performance Excellence were first developed in the late 1980s as a standard of excellence that would help U.S. companies achieve world-class quality. The criteria have continued to evolve over time to reflect changes in management practices and to include the education, health care, and nonprofit (including government) sectors. For more information, see National Institute of Standards and Technology, Baldrige Performance Excellence Program, March 25, 2010, www.nist.gov/baldrige/.

6. Baldrige Performance Excellence Program, Criteria Category 4, Measurement, Analysis, & Knowledge Management.

7. Nancy Allmang and Mylene Ouimette, "Case Study: The NIST Research Library's Experience Using Focus Groups in Strategic Planning," *Library Administration and Management Journal* 21, no. 2 (Spring 2007): 77–82, 94; Harriet Hassler, "What Are Our Customers Reading? An Analysis of the Most Frequently Used Subjects of the NIST Research Library Book Collection Based on Circulation," NISTIR 7205 (Gaithersburg, MD: National Institute of Standards and Technology, 2005); Paula Deutsch and Barbara Silcox, "From Data to Outcomes: Assessment Activities at the NIST Research Library," *Information Outlook* 7, no. 10 (2003): 24–31.

8. Baldrige Performance Excellence Program, Criteria Category 1, Leadership.

XUEMAO WANG AND
EMILY THORNTON
Emory University Libraries,
Atlanta, Georgia

6
Pursuing Organizational Performance Excellence

The Emory University Libraries' Journey

EMORY UNIVERSITY IS A TOP-TWENTY RESEARCH UNIVERSITY in Atlanta, Georgia, with nine academic divisions serving approximately 7,500 undergraduate students, 6,500 graduate students, and 3,000 faculty members. The Emory Libraries support the university's mission "to create, preserve, teach and apply knowledge in the service of humanity" with resources and programs that promote interdisciplinary scholarship and academic excellence on the graduate and undergraduate level; distinctive collections that attract outstanding students, faculty, and staff; technology-rich spaces and digital tools that enable new forms of scholarship; public programs and exhibitions that help connect Emory University with its larger community; and by preserving rare materials that document the full range of the human condition.

The Emory Libraries began to explore and pursue its journey of organizational performance excellence in 2006, when a new vice provost and director of libraries joined the Emory team. This initiative is intended to answer challenging questions that today's higher education and research libraries face, specifically in the areas of organizational value proposition, operational efficiency, and accountability, by establishing an integrated framework and set of assessment tools to understand our organizational strengths and opportunities for continuous improvement. Our goal is to continuously improve the value of library and information services to users, to improve overall organizational effectiveness and competitiveness, and to promote continuous organizational and personal learning.

The Emory Libraries' organizational performance excellence initiative is a journey that is still in the early stages. As with any journey, we have had successes and lessons to learn. This chapter describes our experience by setting our journey in an organizational context, outlining major milestones and accomplishments, summarizing lessons learned, and providing future directions. The first section provides historical context and illustrates our libraries' early attempts at organizational performance excellence. It discusses rationales for our organization's decision to adapt the Baldrige Criteria for Performance Excellence. The second section introduces the Baldrige framework, including our libraries' effort to conduct a high-level self-assessment by creating an organizational profile. It also discusses our efforts to address the questions posed in the seven categories of the Baldrige Criteria framework, plus lessons learned along the way. The final section summarizes our views on the challenges for integrating the Baldrige framework and the future direction of our libraries' organizational performance excellence effort.

Introducing Organizational Performance Excellence, 2006–2009

Prior to his tenure at the Emory Libraries, our vice provost and director of libraries served as research library director at the Los Alamos National Laboratory in New Mexico. There he successfully led his library through a self-assessment using the Baldrige Criteria for Performance Excellence, a framework that promotes continuous improvement by focusing on the customer using an integrated management system approach and data to achieve measurable results. The Los Alamos National Laboratory's Research Library applied for and won the New Mexico state-level Baldrige Quality Award in both 1997 and 2000.[1]

When the vice provost and director of libraries arrived at Emory in 2006, he was charged to present a five-year strategic plan to the university's senior leadership and Board of Trustees. To produce a plan for a twenty-first-century model research library, the director introduced a planning process that served as the libraries' first attempt to adopt an organizational performance excellence methodology. A team of representatives, known as the Executive Strategy Group, was selected by the library management group to draft this strategic plan. In addition, an external consultant was retained to guide and expedite the strategic planning process, and ensure that the eventual plan aligned with the already published university-wide strategic plan.

The "Emory University Libraries Strategic Plan 2008–2012: Fostering Courageous Inquiry" was completed in December 2006 and outlined three major goal areas: digital innovations, special collections, and customer-centered library. Within these goal areas, the plan set eight strategic objectives: establish an informatics research center; establish an institute for digital scholarship; build a signature special collections library; strengthen research collections; strengthen the library branch; strengthen digital library services and next-generation systems; build a bridge between today and the twenty-first-century library; and transform library spaces and services. This extremely ambitious plan called for approximately $82 million in one-time costs, as well as approximately $6 million in annual ongoing costs.[2]

Upon the completion of the 2008–2012 strategic plan, the vice provost and director of libraries realized the libraries needed to take bold action to achieve transformational change. This would require a rigorous process to drive and sustain change. He chose to start the Emory Libraries on a journey to pursue organizational performance excellence by introducing process management to the organization. Dubbed the "Business Plan" initiative, the program consisted of unit-based goals and objectives, customer segmentation, process mapping, and action plans. It also focused on measurements and metrics, with regular reporting on progress in key areas of strategic importance.

While the Emory Libraries had established an assessment program prior to 2006, this program was very isolated and had little impact on the Emory Libraries' operational priority setting. A dedicated assessment coordinator position oversaw most assessment projects, collecting, analyzing, and reporting data and information generated from the perspective of library customers and key stakeholders. The assessment program served Emory Libraries' leaders and decision makers, university offices, and external organizations by guiding staff on metrics development and tracking library progress through metrics. The program's main projects were the annual library user survey, establishing and updating a baseline metric for the Emory University scorecard, and managing the ARL annual statistic survey process.

When the Business Plan process was introduced to the Emory Libraries, management decided that a single, isolated assessment effort would not make a significant impact on the organization. The assessment program had to be integrated into a larger Business Plan framework. An external consultant was retained to provide training on process mapping, customer segmentation, and other key business concepts. The Business Plan Core Team was also formed to work with the consultant. An implementation plan outlining the seven fundamental planning, monitoring, and reporting processes required for the Emory

Libraries' strategic and operational success resulted. These seven processes consisted of strategic planning, business planning, performance reporting, change requests, issue management, assessment, and decision support. In previous years, strategic and business planning events had been managed as special projects. The goal of the implementation plan was to develop these special projects into ongoing and recurrent processes, which would create a foundation for accomplishing the libraries' strategic goals over time. The Business Plan Core Team approached each fundamental process with a six-step methodology: develop an initial process design with forms, templates, and guidance; implement the initial design; obtain feedback and implementation data; redesign the process as indicated; re-implement the process, forms, templates, and guidance; and document the process. This methodology created and maintained a continuous improvement loop for each process.[3]

Introducing the Baldrige Criteria for Performance Excellence, 2009–2010

In 2009, the new position of associate vice provost was created to support the work of the vice provost and director of libraries. Arriving in early 2009, the new associate vice provost is responsible for overseeing the day-to-day library operations and leading and continuing to enhance the organizational performance excellence initiative. The associate vice provost quickly conducted an organizational-wide series of interviews on the status and progress of multiple management processes that had already been implemented. Observing gaps in the staff's understanding of the Business Plan initiative, he placed a high priority on achieving organizational buy-in. The associate vice provost retained the external consultant, but redefined the consultant's role to emphasize designing the architecture for the Business Plan initiative, rather than leading its execution. He replaced the Business Plan Core Team with the Business Process Support Team (BPST), recruiting team members from each major library operational unit to obtain diverse perspectives. The BPST assumed responsibility for coordinating and supporting the implementation of the Emory Libraries Strategic Plan and was given three priority agendas: (1) increase staff buy-in for the business planning practice, facilitate communication, and assist library management in executing the business planning process; (2) simplify the business planning process and make it more applicable to the libraries' operations; and (3) align the libraries' business planning process with its strategic goals and objectives.

The library business planning process improved markedly in the eighteen months of the BPST's existence. Annual guidelines and workbooks produced by the team helped library leaders and managers to write cohesive business plans. Organizational buy-in improved and the annual business planning process was streamlined.

The associate vice provost, however, concluded that the Emory Libraries needed a larger framework that could integrate the libraries' various performance and quality improvement initiatives. With the endorsement of the vice provost and director of libraries, the associate vice provost decided to introduce and establish the Baldrige Criteria for Performance Excellence as the organization's overall framework for performance excellence. The intent was not to pursue the Baldrige National Quality Award, but rather to use the Baldrige Framework to conduct a series of self-assessments on the libraries' improvement efforts. The associate vice provost also planned to use the framework to improve communication, productivity, and effectiveness and achieve the libraries' strategic goals by identifying strengths and opportunities for improvement, providing a common language for improvement, guiding organizational planning and learning, measuring performance and planning in an uncertain environment, and implementing a Balanced Scorecard approach.

The Baldrige Criteria for Performance Excellence provide a continuous improvement framework that is focused on the customer, led by management, based on facts and data, and directed toward results. As one management consulting firm describes it, the Baldrige Framework defines what constitutes quality and performance excellence.[4] It projects clear values, and it measures both qualitative and quantitative aspects of performance and quality management systems. The Baldrige Framework is compatible with different approaches and systems, and it can apply to any organization of any size or type.

While the Emory Libraries have experimented with several other performance metrics systems in the past, the Baldrige Criteria for Performance Excellence is the first comprehensive framework used throughout the entire organization. The Baldrige criteria provide discipline and a way to apply the Emory Libraries' business planning processes across the entire organization. Additionally, the Baldrige framework has been proven to work in many not-for-profit academic settings.

Several key staff members, including the associate vice provost, the senior director of the Content Division, the senior director of the Services Division, the associate director of the Content Division/director for digital assets strategies, the director of finance, the library assessment coordinator, the web strategist, the science librarian, a librarian from the Woodruff Health Science Center Library, and the Metadata and Advanced Cataloging team leader, attended Baldrige conferences and workshops at the state, regional, and national level beginning in 2009.

The Self-Assessment, 2010–present

To begin our Baldrige journey, the libraries' senior management group assigned "champions" to each category of the Baldrige Framework, including leadership; strategic planning; customer focus; measurement, analysis, and knowledge management; workforce focus; operations focus; and results. (See figure 6.1.) The Organizational Profile anchors the Baldrige framework, providing an overview of an organization's mission, governance structure, internal and external business operating environment, products and services, core competencies, and workforce demographics.

Writing a meaningful Organizational Profile, especially for the first time, is a very rigorous exercise. An organization can learn a great deal about itself, its workings, and its position in the market. For the Emory Libraries, the exercise of writing the Organizational Profile provided a good starting foundation and a quick top-level overall assessment of the libraries' current state. It exposed areas where the libraries had insufficient data, as well as areas where

FIGURE 6.1

Framework for the Baldrige Criteria for Performance Excellence

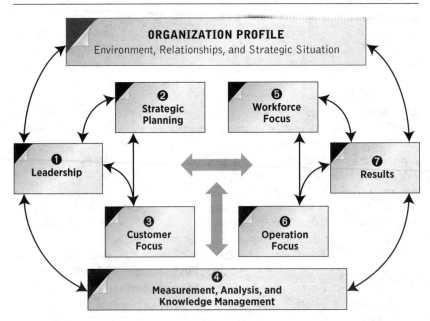

Source: Baldrige Performance Excellence Program. *2011–2012 Criteria for Performance Excellence.* Gaithersburg, MD: National Institute of Standards and Technology, 2011.

performance improvement was required. Statistics gathered for the workforce demographics section, for example, confirmed an underrepresentation of minority librarians, as well as an upcoming increase in retirements that would need to be addressed. Competition for skilled employees with advanced capabilities in information science and knowledge management is also intense.

After work on the Organizational Profile was completed, the libraries chose to focus on the *leadership* category next because of its unquestionable importance. The associate vice provost led this assessment, working with a consultant to customize the criteria questions for an academic library. He interviewed all senior managers and reported the key findings back to the senior management group. Results identified major gaps in leadership development and improvement. One major issue was the lack of clarity around the underlying purpose and authority of the senior management group. There was general confusion about whether the group's role was decision making, consultation, or advisement. Also, there was a perception that communication between the senior management group and the staff was vague and top-down. Finally, several leaders felt that the senior management group should set a better example in the business-planning process. The group had no business plan and did not report out to the organization. Overall, the key findings of this interview process indicated that the senior management group needed to communicate effectively, demonstrate exemplary leadership, and exhibit true teamwork.

In November 2010, the libraries began to address questions in the customer focus category of the framework by choosing to implement a "Voice of the Customer" (VOC) process. Spearheaded by the Services division, VOC takes a systematic and centralized approach to gather, analyze, and document the needs, expectations, outcomes, and desires of the libraries' core customers. The libraries purchased LibPAS to support this initiative, viewing the service as a potential central repository for storing and sharing customer data. Work to refine and improve process mapping in the Emory Libraries is also part of this project, since understanding customer outcomes of a process is critical.

There has been limited effort and resulting progress in applying the Baldrige criteria for self-assessment in the measurement, analysis, and knowledge management category. Throughout the business planning initiative, the libraries conducted exercises to identify organization-wide key performance indicators and asked each unit to identify key measurement metrics. While an example of unit-level metrics might include the ordered or received dates for new items in the acquisitions department, it has been extremely challenging to identify key performance indicators for the overall organization. Several important questions must be answered in order to set valid metrics. For example, what key metrics can truly measure a library's impact in today's academic enterprise? How can one articulate the library's transaction-based metrics to support an argument of the library's impact? What kinds of data management, statistical analysis, and technology infrastructure are required to support robust organizational knowledge management?

Work is ongoing in applying the Baldrige criteria for self-assessment in the categories of strategic planning, workforce focus, and operations focus. The Business Plan initiative is still in use, addressing many of the criteria in the operations focus category of the framework. The revised "Emory University Libraries Strategic Plan 2012–2015: Fostering Courageous Inquiry" was completed in 2011. While the three goal areas identified in the 2008–2012 plan—digital innovations, special collections, and customer-centered library—were retained, more focused strategic objectives were created. These objectives are now better aligned with the organization's core competencies and capabilities, and represent executable initiatives tied to specific resources, time lines, metrics, and outcomes.[5]

While the Emory Libraries has started a self-assessment using all seven categories of the Baldrige criteria, because of uneven progress in each Baldrige category, the libraries still lack an integrated approach. The Emory Libraries joined the Association of Research Libraries' Balanced Scorecard initiative in 2011 in hope of addressing this. The Balanced Scorecard is a business strategy approach that emphasizes the use of metrics to tie actions directly into strategic goals. The Emory Libraries' initial impression of the Scorecard was that it would help us to overcome our difficulties in identifying measurement metrics. As we learn more about this tool, however, we are realizing that the Balanced Scorecard is not just about the metrics, but rather another complicated management framework. This inevitably raises questions about how the Balanced Scorecard may fit into our efforts to apply the Baldrige Framework.[6]

Conclusion: Integration, Communication, and Wider Engagement, 2012–Future

The Emory Libraries' journey toward organizational performance excellence continues. From the beginning, we understood it would be a long journey. Most Baldrige Award-winning organizations realize transformational change after five to seven years. Discipline and an integrated system for continuous improvement are required to realize this change, especially as most employees are eager to see progress and a final outcome when an organization begins its journey toward performance excellence. Thus, patience, endurance, and well-managed expectations are required of everyone involved.

Looking back on our journey, we have learned that an integrative, systematic approach must be introduced, instituted, and disciplined in the early stages of implementing a performance excellence program. Without integration, an organization may develop many different processes in silos, which can soon expand out of control. Integration is hard work, requiring discipline, as well as deeper organization engagement. Integration tests the organization's abilities not only in planning, but also in execution. It requires wider collaboration among all units of the organization. Further, while the traditional academic culture is averse to change, broad organizational buy-in is critical. Without buy-in, a performance excellence initiative's impact will be minimized. Results will not be realized, even though many processes have been implemented and running.

Measuring our library's impact on academic missions continues to be challenging. The identification of key performance indicators, while difficult, is necessary. Such measures must reflect the library's transformational change, especially as it is moving from a traditional collection-centric role, with transaction accounting, to a services-centric role, with impact accounting. Our greatest challenge, however, has been establishing an excellence-driven organizational culture. This requires strong leadership, in addition to cultivating a group of "maverick" or "change agent" employees throughout the organization.

NOTES

1. New Mexico Quality Awards, "Quality New Mexico, List of Recipients, 2009 through 1994," www.qualitynewmexico.org/pdfs/nmqa-2009-1994.pdf.
2. Emory University Libraries, "Emory University Libraries Strategic Plan 2008–2012: Fostering Courageous Inquiry," December 2006.
3. J. Heimel, "Emory University Libraries Strategic and Business Planning: FY08 Process Implementation Plan and Documentation" (internal business document, 2008).
4. Moore Quality Incorporated, "The Baldrige Framework," www.mqi.com/mbnqa.htm.
5. Emory University Libraries, "Strategic Plan of the Emory University Libraries 2012–2015," http://web.library.emory.edu/about/mission-and-strategic-plan.
6. Martha Kyrillidou, "Research Library Issues," No. 271 (August 2010), www.arl.org/resources/pubs/rli/archive/rli271.shtml.

DANA THOMAS AND KATE DAVIS

Scholars Portal/Ontario Council
of University Libraries

7

The Development of an Evaluation and Assessment Program for the Ontario Council of University Libraries

IN JANUARY 2010, THE ONTARIO COUNCIL OF UNIVERSITY LIBRAR-
ies (OCUL) recruited an evaluation and assessment librarian to work with
Scholars Portal, a shared technology infrastructure that provides access to
a suite of information resources and services collected and shared by OCUL
member institutions. This position was the culmination of an increasing focus
within OCUL on evaluation activities and the start of a formal evaluation and
assessment program.

OCUL is a consortium of Ontario's twenty-one university libraries, and
serves a total population of 419,949 faculty and students. OCUL enhances
information services in Ontario through collective purchasing and shared
digital information infrastructure, ensuring that the information tools and
resources essential for high-quality education and research are available in
Ontario's universities.

In early 2000, OCUL largely focused on library collection activities such
as consortial resource purchasing. With the growing importance of technology and e-resources in academic libraries, however, the consortium started
to consider what benefits could be derived from approaching these changes

collectively. OCUL responded by expanding its activities to include collaborative planning; research; professional development and advocacy; and by establishing the Scholars Portal Operation Team. It was OCUL's hope that this team of information professionals focused on developing innovative digital library services would ensure rapid and reliable response time for information services and resources; provide for the long-term, secure archiving of resources to ensure continued availability; create a network of intellectual resources by linking ideas, materials, and documents; and provide a malleable environment that fosters additional innovation in response to the needs of users. The Scholars Portal Operation Team is currently comprised of eleven librarians and thirteen technical staff.

The foundations of Scholars Portal were laid in 2001, when OCUL created an interlibrary loan and journal archiving and access system. Both systems were noteworthy because they were locally managed rather than hosted by commercial vendors. The journal system, however, was quite unique. It was designed as a simple, straightforward model for journal archiving. Journal content was acquired from publishers and loaded on a locally administered system, pioneering an "open or light archive" model that combined long-term preservation functions with current user access needs.

Ten years later, the Scholars Portal journals platform now contains over 30,000,000 journal articles, representing over 12,000 journals and more than twenty academic publishers. The Scholars Portal suite of resources and services has also expanded, with a local installation of RefWorks and SFX in 2004, and federated searching of locally loaded databases in 2005. By 2011, Scholars Portal offered additional local platforms for e-books, microdata, and geospatial data. It also added a virtual reference service.

While locally stored content and locally managed software serve as the cornerstone of Scholars Portal activities and continue to provide enormous benefits to OCUL institutions, as Scholars Portal reached its ten-year anniversary, a growing need to demonstrate these benefits to community stakeholders was recognized, along with a need to ensure that the development of Scholars Portal was based on users' requirements. These two factors were the basis of the evaluation and assessment program.

In this chapter, we describe the history of evaluation and assessment within OCUL and describe how the formal evaluation and assessment program was established. We detail the staff and other resources needed for the program and highlight key evaluation and assessment projects that illustrate how the program facilitated an overall shift in focus within OCUL from gathering data as needed to using data proactively for advocacy and service improvement. Lastly, we discuss how the program itself is evolving, how it is influencing the development of existing services, and how it has changed the questions we ask as we build new services.

History of Evaluation and Assessment at OCUL

OCUL's first collaborative effort to evaluate its services and resources occurred during the 2004–2005 academic year, when it utilized the Measuring the Impact of Networked Electronic Services (MINES for Libraries) survey instrument to evaluate the success of the Scholars Portal program.[1] OCUL was particularly interested in investigating the MINES for Libraries survey's potential as part of an overall assessment strategy for Scholars Portal, in conjunction with use data and other methods for gathering user feedback. The survey ran for a year within the scope of the Scholars Portal journals platform and results were distributed to OCUL member libraries' directors and librarians. A day of presentations was also held to highlight the results, insights gained, and potential future implications. Three years later, however, little else had been done and the OCUL community needed to confront a number of challenges for which evaluation was essential.

The economic climate of 2008 had created significant financial pressures on OCUL member institutions, resulting in stagnant or shrinking budgets for OCUL member libraries. These budgetary constraints made it imperative to ensure that the investments OCUL member libraries were making in e-resources were based on a clear understanding of what contents were included in a product and how a product was being used by library patrons. Both usage statistics and a detailed analysis of content overlap were required to ensure that library staff were making informed decisions about canceling existing products or purchasing new products.

Meanwhile, library services and resources continued to be revolutionized by changes in how information is made available on the Internet. The technology on which the Scholars Portal journals platform operated was starting to show its age and needed to be replaced. Scholars Portal was also beginning to integrate different types of content, and library vendors were beginning to develop discovery systems that promised to allow searchers access to the majority of library content from a single, easy-to-use interface. The expectations and research needs of OCUL's user community further continued to change with the adoption of social networking and user-created content.

In order to address these challenges, OCUL hired external consultants to conduct user focus groups that would inform development of a new platform and interface for the local journals system and future developments relating to discovery layers and the broader search environment. These sessions were intended to help OCUL and the Scholars Portal team to better understand the information research process of experienced researchers, the tools and techniques researchers currently employ, and researchers' vision for an "ideal" information research process. Scholars Portal staff and OCUL community members worked with the consultants to establish objectives and methodology for the sessions and to recruit participants. The feedback obtained was used to validate a framework of research stages to be considered in all Scholars Portal development projects and identified numerous opportunities for better supporting information research processes. Given the success of the initial sessions, it was decided that user research had to be an ongoing aspect of the development of Scholars Portal.

The Evaluation and Assessment Librarian

With the growth of Scholars Portal resources and services there was a huge volume of usage data that was largely unanalyzed because the Scholars Portal team lacked both contextual knowledge to make sense of all the numbers and a central person to coordinate evaluation and assessment activities. Individual OCUL member libraries had similar sets of data for products from commercial vendors that were similarly underused. While the external consultants had extensive expertise in conducting research into user needs, they did not have the expertise required to evaluate OCUL's e-resources or to lead a number of necessary usage initiatives identified by OCUL and Scholars Portal staff. Electronic resources and serials librarians, whose work would most naturally include electronic resource evaluation, were already finding their professional portfolios exploding with new responsibilities as innovative technology continued to transform digital library services.

Recognizing the need to dedicate staff time to evaluation and assessment activities and that the expertise required to complete these activities could only be found within the OCUL community, the OCUL executive agreed to fund a new position on the Scholars Portal team. The evaluation and assessment librarian would be charged with creating a solution for usage data and collection overlap analysis. This included developing a usage portal that would identify overlap of content between different commercial resources; identify overlap of content between Scholars Portal Search and other resources; offer comprehensive usage information for Scholars Portal and commercial providers; and provide data related to costs. The librarian would also be responsible for conducting internal and external environmental scans to determine needs within the consortia and evaluation and assessment practices among other libraries and consortia; researching the COUNTER compliance status of consortial vendors; identifying resources and tools for assessment that are freely available from commercial vendors; communicating with the OCUL member library community; and providing training related to the Scholars Portal evaluation and assessment program. This librarian would also provide advice for small projects led by other Scholars Portal team members and help to develop statistics to communicate the value of Scholars Portal to stakeholders within the consortium, design user surveys, develop quality assurance procedures, and provide discovery layer assessment.

The Evaluation and Assessment Program

A major component of OCUL's work revolves around collections. The consortium licenses electronic resources that include abstracting and indexing databases, e-journal packages, full-text aggregator databases, and e-book collections. Content is locally loaded when OCUL has successfully negotiated load rights with vendors, giving subscribing institutions dual access for resources—on the vendor's native platform and on the Scholars Portal platform. In contrast to some other regional consortia in the United States, OCUL's licensing activities are conducted on an opt-in basis, meaning consortial deals can involve as few as three OCUL member libraries, or all twenty-one. Since all OCUL members are also part of the Canadian Research Knowledge Network (CRKN), a national consortium, and CRKN always has at least one OCUL member on their Negotiations Resource Team, local loading is also negotiated to meet Ontario's needs wherever possible. Resources licensed by CRKN and OCUL include major publisher collections such as Wiley and Elsevier, and large indexing databases, such as PsycINFO, Web of Science, and SCOPUS. We also subscribe consortially to aggregator databases from EBSCO, ProQuest, and Gale. For some member institutions, consortial resources represent the bulk of their total electronic resource collection, and for other, larger institutions, these resources are only a small to medium component of their overall e-resource expenditures. Within this context, there are several major issues of importance, especially involving usage and overlap analysis for collection development and evaluation. Recent projects involve the creation of the Scholars Portal Usage Data portal, a second MINES for Libraries survey, and the development of a Serials Collection Overlap Tool.

COUNTER Compliance and the Scholars Portal Usage Data Portal

For as long as libraries have existed, usage data, whether for physical or electronic resources, has been a part of the librarian's toolkit for evaluating the importance of titles in their collections. In the electronic environment, the technical ability to track use in ways and in depths not possible in the print environment only stimulated librarians' appetite for more and better data on which to base collection evaluation and decision making. In the early days of online resources, each vendor tracked "downloads" or "views" differently.

There was little control for removing unintentional uses, such as double clicks, from the usage data or counting a click through from an HTML to a PDF format of an article as one use. This lack of standardization in tracking and reporting usage meant that libraries could not compare use of one vendor's product to another vendor's product. Reports were instead generally used to track an overall trend in use that could answer only basic questions, such as: "Has use of vendor X's product increased since last year?" or "I need to cancel something. What product is decreasing in usage?"

Project COUNTER, or Counting the Use of Networked Electronic Resources, emerged to address the demand for comparable and reliable usage data within the library community.[2] First released in 2003, the COUNTER code of practice provided a standard for database and e-journal vendors to follow that established clear guidelines for counting and reporting use in a consistent manner. Vendors compliant with the COUNTER code must undergo rigorous testing and external audits at periodic time intervals to ensure that the usage statistics they provide remain in compliance with the code. Now in its third release for journals and databases, COUNTER has been widely adopted, with 139 vendors officially compliant with the code and 37 with the more recently developed code for books and reference works. While recognizing that COUNTER use data is still not perfect, librarians embrace it because it allows them to make cross-vendor use comparisons with reasonable confidence that the numbers are in fact comparable.

The Scholars Portal journals platform was established in 2002 and provides a collection of more than 12,000 locally loaded, consortially licensed e-journal titles. OCUL controls the design of and improvements to the interface, conducts usability studies with its user community, and strives to seamlessly integrate other services such as RefWorks into the platform. Many OCUL member libraries choose to point their users to the Scholars Portal journals platform as an interdisciplinary, full-text research database. They also direct OpenURL requests for specific articles to the Scholars Portal journals platform. Though the Scholars Portal platform has many benefits, some drawbacks such as time lags can occur as OCUL obtains content from publishers for loading. Supplemental data is also sometimes missing and the portal lacks the unique functionality of some native vendor platforms, meaning that most OCUL member libraries still also direct users to the native vendor interfaces. Having dual access points results in two sets of use data to collect, analyze, and report.

Fortunately for the evaluation and assessment program, most of OCUL's consortial vendors are COUNTER-compliant. Further, some of the noncompliant vendors the consortium works with offer "counter style" reports, meaning that their data can be technically compared, but is not officially compliant. Thus, to integrate and address the dual sets of data resulting from allowing users to access resources through the Scholars Portal journals platform and native vendor interfaces, it was decided to seek COUNTER compliance for the Scholars Portal platform.

A team consisting of the evaluation and assessment librarian, the project manager for e-books, the Scholars Portal director, a senior systems developer, and books and journals programmers was formed a month after the decision was reached to become familiar with the COUNTER code of practice, instructions to vendors, and the process for achieving compliance. The team met several times to discuss definitions within the code that required clarification, how the team should interpret the relevance of the code's definitions to our Scholars Portal system, and our stats-logging procedures for the Scholars Portal platform. Once the team was confident that our counting was compliant with the COUNTER code of practice to the best of our understanding, our senior systems developer created an online portal on which we could store use data and provide the download options specified by the COUNTER code of practice, including .xls, .csv, and .xml formats. This portal was designed as a simple, clear interface for retrieving use data for books and journals and is now known as SPUD (Scholars Portal Usage Data). While we worked on obtaining COUNTER-compliant status, we provided COUNTER-style reports for journals and books to OCUL staff and member libraries.

Over the next several months, a library test site identified by Project COUNTER examined our platform and reports and identified several items for us to address. We then identified an auditor to work with who performed additional tests, leading to additional refinements. Eventually, three of our four reports received a passing grade. Two were for journals and two were for books. The COUNTER code of practice for logging usage data for journals and databases was much easier for us to interpret and apply to the Scholars Portal platform. The COUNTER code of practice for books and reference works was more difficult to apply as the COUNTER code offers two different options for counting book usage. Book report one counts title uses and book report two, section uses. With the COUNTER project director, we determined that book report two would be more relevant for our platform, as we could identify uses at a more granular level than title. Book report two specifies "section" use for each e-book title. The code guides vendors producing book report two to count chapters as sections wherever possible. When this level cannot be used for the section, however, other sections such as pages were deemed acceptable at the time we were developing our COUNTER reports. After discovering this, we began to question the value in producing this report, as we realized it did not support cross-vendor comparability in the same way as the journal and database reports. Further, e-books are still relatively young and vendors have yet to develop widely accepted standards for, among others, digital rights management, e-book readers, and file formats. The COUNTER code of practice for books and reference works will continue to evolve to accommodate changes in technology, user behavior, and information professionals' evaluation needs. Because the Scholars Portal e-book platform was designed to accommodate many reading options, including single-page views, two-page views, and pdf section extracts, however, we also realized we would be unable to produce a book report that could meet the code's requirements. Despite this minor failure, we considered the overall project a success.

Achieving COUNTER compliance was a major step forward in our consortium's ability to evaluate resources on an organized, ongoing basis. First, because respected industry standards are now followed, member libraries can have confidence in the use reports provided by OCUL staff. While Scholars Portal has been producing non-COUNTER use data and sharing it using various platform solutions since its journals platform was first available in 2002, following the COUNTER standard may instill more confidence in the calculations used to communicate the value of journals to consortium members. Second, at both the consortial and local levels, librarians are now able to merge use between the Scholars Portal and native vendor platforms to establish a single figure for journals accessed via both platforms. Previously, two reports were provided but could not be compared or combined. We now have a single, reliable metric that we can use as a true indicator of total journal use for OCUL licenses. Third, the COUNTER standard has been incorporated into the design of other library systems, such as electronic resource management systems (ERMs), and statistics aggregation tools, such as Scholarly Stats, 360 Counter, and UStat. By offering use data in the COUNTER format, OCUL member libraries can load the Scholars Portal data into these products, combine it with COUNTER data from other vendors, and compare it with price information, facilitating cost per use calculations.

Our next step is to become a SUSHI, or Standarized Usage Statistics Harvesting Initiative vendor. SUSHI "defines an automated request and response model for the harvesting of electronic resource usage data utilizing a Web services framework."[3] By offering our members a SUSHI account for harvesting usage, they will be able to automatically import data into ERMs and other systems that can ingest COUNTER use data. Automating in this way significantly reduces staff time, as downloading and uploading COUNTER reports is somewhat time-intensive. ERMs and statistical aggregation tools providing SUSHI harvesting offer significant time savings as basic reports can easily be generated. This liberates library staff to focus on the more important function of analyzing the results rather than merely compiling and reporting the data.

All OCUL member librarians now have access to the UStat statistical aggregation tool, since Ex Libris, the vendor for SFX, now offers this product free of charge to SFX customers. UStat can automatically harvest COUNTER journal reports, ingest COUNTER journal and database reports uploaded by a customer, and create reports broken down by title, platform, publisher, database, and subscriber. UStat also automatically creates bar and line charts showing trends over time, and the most popular journals, platforms, and databases. With no storage limit on the amount of use data and a recent development that includes cost per use reporting, this tool has the potential to provide the means to effectively and efficiently explore journal and database use. Similar benefits could be enjoyed by any library using any software that ingests COUNTER data.

A Second Iteration of MINES for Libraries at OCUL

MINES for Libraries surveys uses of electronic resources by intercepting users as they connect with library resources through a proxy server, campus router, or in OCUL's case, its SFX OpenURL link resolver.[4] MINES for Libraries was first selected to run during the 2004–2005 academic year as a way to learn more about how our user community was finding out about particular resources and for what purposes they were using them. The consortium was also interested in discovering whether MINES for Libraries could offer a way to "make studies of patron usage of OCUL networked electronic resources routine, robust, and integrated into decision making."[5]

Five years later, as an interest in library assessment resurfaced, the OCUL member library directors agreed that it was time to revisit this five-question, point-of-use survey. Some of the key questions of interest to explore included: Could MINES data demonstrate library value? What are the variations in use of resources within the library, on campus outside of the library, and off campus? What are the patterns of use for resources across disciplines and user groups? Why are people using electronic resources? How has use changed since the 2004–2005 survey? Does MINES for Libraries contribute to our continued assessment efforts? Can we use MINES for Libraries to benchmark across libraries? Are there differences in use across publishers, between consortial and local resources, between free and open-access resources, and among types of electronic resources, including e-books, e-journals, and databases?

Once the directors approved of offering the survey during the 2010–2011 academic year, OCUL coordinated with ARL to implement it and produce consortial and institutional reports at the conclusion of the data collection period. The OCUL office and Scholars Portal office, both located within Robarts Library at the University of Toronto, have a convenient partner in the University of Toronto Libraries. The librarians and programmers on the Scholars Portal team worked with the University of Toronto Libraries and programmers within the University of Toronto's Information Technology Services Department to design a script to use with SFX that would trigger the MINES for Libraries survey from within the link resolver, and capture metadata that could later be analyzed. Once the technical aspects of delivering the survey were addressed, OCUL member libraries were asked to participate. While sixteen of the twenty-one OCUL member libraries signed institutional contracts to administer the survey, numerous adjustments were required to allow the MINES for Libraries protocol to address each individual member library's needs while still allowing for cross-institutional comparisons and analysis. Many schools, for example, felt that the ARL-identified subject disciplines were too general to effectively address local needs and analyze survey results. Time was invested to map more granular institutional disciplines, such as veterinary medicine, to ARL's disciplines so that analysis could be done at both levels. Other schools needed the flexibility to offer MINES for Libraries as an optional survey. When MINES for Libraries was administered during the 2004–2005 academic year, the survey was mandatory. Patrons had to complete the brief questionnaire to proceed to their desired resource. This became problematic for many OCUL member libraries, and only five of the sixteen libraries contracting to participate in the 2010–2011 survey could run a mandatory survey. ARL and OCUL worked together to address this by developing mandatory and optional modes for the survey and then tested these modes at the five institutions that could run a mandatory survey to look for statistically significant differences. Though the statistical analysis was not complete at the time of this publication, ARL and OCUL reviewed the descriptive statistics and, noting only small differences, developed reports that combine the results and separate reports for those institutions that implemented both the mandatory and optional modes of the survey. The availability of mandatory and optional modes thus allowed a much broader group of participants in the survey.

Before each participating library's survey went live, webinars and conference calls were held and example documents were distributed to ensure that all local contacts knew what to expect, understood the timing for the start of the data collection, and had an opportunity to ask questions and express concerns. A Google group was established to facilitate hassle-free communication among all parties. Since the survey protocol was intended to run for a full twelve-month period, it was important that public services librarians had an avenue for reporting concerns. At optional mode sites, for example, patrons could click on a link to opt out of the survey and proceed to their desired resource. Since this link was not always easily detected, instructions were created for public services librarians to help them assist patrons who wished to opt out of the survey.

Following the conclusion of the data collection period, the evaluation and assessment librarian then enriched all of the OCUL data by coding the comments; normalizing publisher names and consortial, local, or open-access license types; and adjusting the electronic resource type to e-book, e-journal, database, or other appropriate category to make full use of the metadata provided by SFX along with results of the MINES for Libraries survey. While enriching the data required a significant investment of time and energy, it allowed both the consortium and participating libraries to better understand e-resource use among OCUL member libraries.

After spending a significant amount of time with the data, the evaluation and assessment librarian was afforded an overall picture of the results, perfectly positioning her to communicate the value of the survey and provide ideas, inspiration, and support for other librarians within the consortium interested in conducting their own research. She also provided a model for enriching results to meaningfully impact decision making. While the MINES for Libraries survey provides a useful snapshot of electronic resource use and patron demographics, without the evaluation and assessment librarian's enrichment of the data, questions at a publisher, subscription type, or electronic resource-type level could not be addressed. This granularity made the results much more interesting and meaningful for decision makers. The coded comments also allowed institutions to pick out positive quotations easily for use in discussions with their stakeholders. By using a standard instrument like MINES for Libraries and coordinating efforts so that the whole consortium administered the survey protocol both simultaneously and in a uniform way, OCUL and the participating libraries also gained the ability to benchmark their results against other similar groups of libraries.

The Serials Collection Overlap Tool: Facilitating Evidence-Based Collection Development

The Serials Collection Overlap Tool (SCOT) is a web-based tool that Scholars Portal librarians and staff developed to identify overlapping and unique full-text and indexed titles available in OCUL member libraries' serial holdings. SCOT offers a significant range of comparison options to support collections evaluation activities through a relatively simple, easy-to-use interface. The tool was developed to address the particular needs of member libraries in the absence of a comparable preexisting commercial or freely available product. Specifically, SCOT supports both the work of the consortium as well as that of individual consortium members in assessing collections for overlap, comparing collections for strength in particular subject areas, and weeding print titles available in purchased back file collections and other perpetually licensed collections. By creating this tool within the evaluation and assessment program, librarians within OCUL can now make evidence-supported statements about the degree to which overlap exists in their collections and to demonstrate that the unique content within each product is valuable enough to warrant an otherwise apparent overpayment for the same content. SCOT also allows librarians to see exactly where they may be able to save money on collections while creating the least negative impact on patrons and collections. Finally, SCOT may show where, when funds are available, opportunities exist to expand collections through new acquisitions.

Just as the transition from print to digital brought new challenges and opportunities for the analysis of usage data, so too did it transform vendor relationships and library acquisitions. In the print world, academic libraries had access to far fewer periodical titles and generally managed the purchase of these titles through a subscription agent. Access to and use of print indexes was more limited in comparison to the online databases and indexes we enjoy today. Scholars in a particular discipline used to rely on a single subject-specific index, since research used to be much less interdisciplinary and print indexes required so much of their time. Today, most academic libraries provide access to tens of thousands of electronic journal titles and hundreds of subject-specific and interdisciplinary databases. As publishers began to sell their content through individual subscriptions, as part of journal packages, or through third parties such as content aggregators, like EBSCO, ProQuest, or Gale, libraries began to acquire content in a myriad of different permutations. While some wonderful benefits results from these changes, some challenges also emerged. Libraries now have significant overlap in their coverage of e-journals. Further, with the evolution of Google Scholar, federated search, discovery layers, and interdisciplinary research, the value of subject-specific indexes is no longer clear. With the economic downturn in 2008, and the pressure on libraries to identify cost savings, these issues require investigation. Concern over increases in journal subscription prices and the value and sustainability of "Big Deal" subscription packages also continues. It is within this context that the need for a tool dedicated to the problem of electronic resource collection overlap was identified.

The evaluation and assessment librarian, in her previous position as an electronic resources librarian, looked at many different tools designed for analyzing serial lists for overlapping and unique titles. Through previous experience with SFX, Ulrich's Serials Analysis, and the Colorado Alliance's Gold Rush collection overlap tool, she formed a basic list of features and functionalities and then conducted an external and internal environmental scan to identify the needs of the consortium and OCUL members libraries and other available products.[6] The internal scan revealed that the consortium needed the ability to identify unique and overlapping titles within both citation and full-text holdings to make actionable cancellation and weeding decisions. Most commercial tools provided one type of holdings comparison or the other, and imposed a limit on the number of resources that could be compared at one time. Link resolver tools, such as SFX, were excellent at revealing overlap and unique content in full-text holdings, but lacked any information about indexing and abstracting databases.

Finding that no commercial system or free resource met all of OCUL's requirements, the evaluation and assessment librarian started work on SCOT, an in-house system that would pull holdings data from other systems and would meet OCUL's collection analysis needs. Since OCUL had a consortial implementation of SFX, the full-text holdings for all member libraries could be obtained. The abstracting and indexing serial holdings required obtaining title lists from another source. Gold Rush, a tool from the Colorado Alliance, was licensed for OCUL for this purpose, and an agreement with the Colorado Alliance to import holdings data for indexing and abstracting databases included in Gold Rush was established. In order to then associate these abstracting and indexing databases with subscribing OCUL schools, a project to associate "entitlements" information for Gold Rush titles was assigned to a library school student to complete during the summer months. Once a complete list of all products from Gold Rush and SFX was produced, the evaluation and assessment librarian generated several questions to address after examining the lists: In case of overlap, would SCOT use the holdings from SFX or from Gold Rush? Which products were truly equivalent between the two knowledge bases? What categories or groupings labels should be assigned to facilitate the evaluation of electronic collections? Labels such as free or open access, consortial, publisher package, aggregator database, and abstracting and indexing database were then assigned to the holdings. A *My Databases* and *All Databases* distinction was developed within the tool to allow users to switch between resources within and outside of their local collection. To assist with developing and refining SCOT, a subgroup within the OCUL Information Resources committee, a group that conducts consortial acquisitions-related activities, was formed. The subgroup, with the programmer and the evaluation and assessment librarian, then conducted a series of tests to examine the accuracy of comparisons and ease of use.

Today, SCOT facilitates comparisons of predefined groupings, custom groupings, and individual databases. The tool can also accept uploaded ISSN lists to run comparisons against resources or core subject lists that are not included within the overlap tool's knowledge base. SCOT comparisons can include subscribed or unsubscribed resources, and can be limited by coverage type, such as full text or citation only, and by subject. Up to three groupings, uploaded lists, individual databases, or a combination of any three of the above can be compared. The flexibility in comparison options, along with the inclusion of an *All My Holdings* predefined grouping that includes all of a member library's full-text and abstracting and indexing database holdings, removed the restrictions of many commercial tools that prevented customers from looking at their entire collection. By comparing an unsubscribed database to *All My Holdings*, for example, an OCUL member library can easily see how many unique titles would be added through an acquisition. Conversely, by comparing a subscribed resource against *All My Holdings*, a school could determine how many titles would be lost in a cancellation.

During development, institutional accounts as well as a consortial account were created. The OCUL account includes all of the schools' holdings, allowing comparisons between institutions for purposes such as preparing library reports for program reviews, creating proposals to identify resources for purchase based on peer holdings to support a program, or identifying resources held in common with schools offering similar programs. A feature allowing member libraries to further analyze titles outside of SCOT by exporting data from the system into Microsoft Excel was also developed.

To date, feedback for SCOT has been excellent, although cancellation of holdings has not been occurring widely at OCUL member libraries. SCOT has been used within OCUL for producing reports to allow member libraries to make evidence-based decisions related to the renewal and evaluation of new consortial deals. It has also been used at the local level for several program evaluations. Many Canadian universities have been able to postpone canceling electronic resources due to the strength of the Canadian dollar and by cutting resources and services in other areas. With continuing flat budgets and serials inflation, however, this trend is not sustainable. We expect to see the adoption of SCOT for supporting electronic resource cancellations increase in the coming year. As SCOT continues to develop, planned enhancements for the tool include support for calculating cost per unique title in relation to use, cost to interlibrary loan, and perhaps the inclusion of other contextual information such as a title's impact factor.

Conclusion

The first two years of our formal evaluation and assessment program focused on three main areas: the second implementation of the MINES for Libraries survey; the identification of data collected by Scholars Portal and how it could be leveraged by OCUL and member libraries to demonstrate such things as ROI to stakeholders; and the identification of functional requirements for and the development of data analysis tools such as SCOT and SPUD.

Currently, we are in the process of broadening involvement in the program. Our challenge now is to ensure that librarians within the consortium are effectively utilizing both the tools and the analyses produced by the evaluation and assessment librarian. Presentations, webinars, and on-site training are assisting us in achieving this goal. A systematic approach to using

COUNTER data from SPUD and using SCOT for collection analysis is gradually being incorporated into the regular work of the consortium and member libraries. Moving forward, the more our evaluation and assessment program can succeed in making tools available, easy-to-use, and meaningful, the more we believe we will be successful with evaluation and assessment as a whole.

NOTES

1. MINES for Libraries is a survey protocol designed by Brinley Franklin, vice provost for university libraries, University of Connecticut, and Terry Plum, assistant dean for technology and director of the Simmons Graduate School of Library and Information Science. It is now part of the Association of Research Libraries' StatsQUAL Library Assessment Tools. See "MINES for Libraries: Measuring the Impact of Networked Electronic Services," last modified April 21, 2010, www.arl.org/stats/initiatives/mines/index.shtml.
2. "COUNTER—Counting Online Usage of Networked Electronic Resources," www.projectcounter.org.
3. "Standardized Usage Statistics Harvesting Initiatives (SUSHI)," www.niso.org/workrooms/sushi.
4. There are several MINES for Libraries presentations and publications available to interested readers at www.minesforlibraries.org/publications.
5. Martha Kyrillidou, Toni Olshen, Brinley Franklin, and Terry Plum, "Mines for Libraries: Measuring the Impact of Networked Electronic Services and the Ontario Council of University Libraries' Scholars Portal, Final Report," 2005, www.libqual.org/documents/admin/FINAL%20REPORT_Jan26mk.pdf.
6. Other available collection analysis products include the Joint Information Systems Committee's Academic Database Assessment Tool (www.jisc-adat .com/adat/home.pl), and Serials Solutions' 360 Overlap Analysis Tool (www.serialsolutions.com/en/services/360-core/features/). Several libraries and consortia have also developed in-house tools, including the University of Washington Libraries. See "Database Helps Libraries Manage Journals," http://wsutoday.wsu.edu/pages/Publications.asp?Action=Detail &PublicationID=15305&PageID=21.

KYMBERLY ANNE GOODSON
AND DANIEL SUCHY
University of California, San Diego

8
Creating Analyst Positions in an Academic Library

The UC-San Diego Example

ACADEMIC LIBRARIES ARE FACING INCREASING PRESSURE TO illustrate their value to stakeholders and to justify expenditures, both qualitatively and quantitatively. In response, many have moved toward seeking greater user feedback and performing more holistic and systematic assessments. The use of statistics, data, and other concrete information to inform decisions about staffing, services, resources, facilities, and more is increasing, as evidenced in part by the growing popularity of the biennial Library Assessment Conference.[1] ALA conference sessions such as "Using Today's Numbers to Plan Tomorrow's Services: Effective User Services Assessment" and "Maybe It Has Already Been Done: Locating Existing Data for Planning, Assessment, and Advocacy" are also increasing, providing information on data-driven and evidence-based decision making using a wide range of assessment methodologies and applications.[2]

The University of California, San Diego (UCSD) enrolls roughly 23,000 undergraduate and 4,000 graduate students and is particularly noted for its engineering, science, math, and biology programs.[3] The UCSD Libraries, composed of six separate libraries housed within three buildings both on and off campus, support the university's faculty, students, and medical staff. In the fall of 2007, the libraries' associate university librarian for user services (AUL/ user services) established a new decision support analyst position that would report directly to her. Prior to 2007, while some statistics related to library operations and resources were readily available and reported regularly, others were not. Much of the libraries' data were disorganized, incomplete, or scattered in multiple locations, formats, or technologies. The libraries' statistics-gathering efforts were complicated by a lack of consistency for recording data across library locations, leaving administrators to make difficult decisions with often limited, incomplete, or potentially biased information.

A complementary user services technology analyst position was created in 2009. Today the decision support and user services technology analyst positions now provide decision support and technology planning and implementation services for the UCSD Libraries. They also facilitate more systematic and sustained assessment and analysis efforts within the libraries' user services areas and, in some instances, more broadly across the organization. This chapter highlights the evolution of the analyst position model at the UCSD Libraries, and outlines the responsibilities of the decision support and user services technology analysts. It then provides examples of projects assigned to each analyst and considerations for other library organizations thinking of implementing an analyst model.

Evolution of the Analyst Position Model: The UCSD Libraries' Solution

Despite the trend toward greater use of assessment results, data analysis, and evidence-based information in decision making, many academic libraries continue to lack the staff to support these increasing demands. In 2007 UCSD Libraries' administrators, recognizing the growing importance of assessment and the lack of a dedicated individual, department, or committee to perform many of these tasks, began to consider how assessment-related activities could be accomplished and sustained long-term. Rather than developing an assessment committee or centralized assessment office, as other academic libraries have chosen, administrators decided to establish analyst positions with specialized roles, including assessment. Additionally, because funding to support new positions was unavailable, existing employees were targeted to assume these new responsibilities.

The AUL/user services established the decision support analyst position first, moving the assistant director for access services in the Social Sciences & Humanities Library into the role half-time in the fall of 2007. Primary responsibilities for the new position included planning and conducting assessments and performing a variety of other studies and analyses to facilitate effective, data-driven decision making. While the librarian moving into this position had skills related to project management and analysis that qualified her for the work, she had to learn new skills related to usability and other assessment methodologies. After a one-year pilot, the value of the decision support analyst's work was assessed, and a decision was made to not only continue, but to increase the position to full-time status. This was accomplished by the summer of 2009.

When the decision support analyst position was established, the AUL/user services noted that her intention was to provide herself and the libraries' administrative team with the support needed to make well-informed, data-driven decisions. She further elaborated that nearly any service or project could be assigned to the decision support analyst for analysis. While the exact details of the decision support analyst role evolved over time, the individual in the position was charged to lead various user services-related projects assigned to her by library administration, manage the timelines and progress of these projects, and monitor selected statistics impacting user services to track the performance of the library's established public services. The decision support analyst currently researches and summarizes assigned issues and topics, conducts comparisons among University of California and ARL libraries, and evaluates the libraries against national, regional, and local benchmarks. She conducts various types of usability and usage studies and collects data for statistical and budgetary analyses. The decision support analyst is responsible for conducting internal and external research, documenting findings, and establishing facts. She must be able to draw valid conclusions and make appropriate recommendations. The analyst generates reports as requested and provides the libraries' administration with data, analysis, and materials for presentations and reports. The analyst is responsible for providing supplemental information that enhances administrators' ability to make appropriate decisions. She must facilitate positive working relationships with library staff and external contacts, collaborating when needed.

The success of the decision support analyst position, partnered with the realization that additional user services–related technology projects and assessments needed to be pursued, led to the creation of the user services technology analyst position. This role, initially set at quarter-time, was assigned to the Social Sciences & Humanities Library's electronic information services coordinator. As projects and duties for this position grew, the incumbent's former responsibilities were reassigned to others and the position was increased to full-time status by late 2009.

The user services technology analyst position, while created to work within the UCSD Libraries' specific environment, is a hybrid of positions found both in academia and the private sector. Libraries rely heavily on their information technology operations to support research and instructional services, as well as public and staff computing. The libraries' user services staff, through their training, daily interaction with users, and expert knowledge of library trends, are often best equipped to predict changes in existing services that may require technology or information technology (IT) support. IT staff in turn must make projects proposed by or initiated by user services staff a reality.

Strained communication and relations between IT staff and librarians, however, are not uncommon. In 2010 at least two webcasts, "Strengthening the IT/Library Staff Partnership" and "Strategic Planning for Library-IT Collaboration," addressed this issue.[4] In academic libraries, a process for guiding new user services/IT projects from conception to completion is often absent. Usually libraries have a positive "problem" in that more forward-thinking technology project ideas are generated than can be implemented. Having numerous competing ideas without a process to prioritize projects in regard to feasibility, scope, or available resources or a process to identify and structure project requirements, however, can derail new initiatives. The lack of a formal project manager can also jeopardize a project's success.

The user services technology analyst facilitates a collaborative working relationship between user services staff and IT, working to implement a structured process for clearly identifying project requirements, or the features and functions that should be built into a new technology service or product. The analyst serves as a "translator" between what user services staff desire and what is technically possible. In this role, the analyst ensures that a project does not become unmanageable.

The user services technology analyst must have a user-oriented background and possess firsthand knowledge of and experience working with technology. An ability to communicate effectively with both IT professionals and librarians and administrators in user services is essential, along with an understanding of the perspectives of each group. This position is responsible for providing the administration with various types of technology analyses, needs assessments, and usability study reviews. In addition, the user services technology analyst serves as a technology liaison or consultant to various library committees and groups to communicate new technology services and changes across the organization. The analyst is also expected to work closely with the libraries' IT units to manage and implement changes to library public computing.

The decision support analyst initially worked alone, interfacing with various groups and individuals as projects required, and meeting individually with the AUL/user services to receive direction and report on project progress. Once the user services technology analyst assumed his role full-time, the analysts became a collaborative team, working together on library-wide projects and meeting regularly with the AUL/user services to report on progress, receive and prioritize project assignments, and surface ideas and concerns for consideration or discussion.

Both analysts serve on various library committees and task groups and take action as appropriate to expand awareness of library developments at UCSD and elsewhere. They also communicate their findings, research, or other information through the sharing of textual, visual, or statistical reports and through presentations to various management and library-wide groups, as requested or appropriate.

Typical Project Life Cycle

Projects assigned to the analysts that involve new or significantly modified services, technologies, resources, and practices often require a variety of actions. A project may typically begin with an analyst conducting a literature review or environmental scan to better understand existing options or practices. Feedback to library administration is then provided, so administrators may consider the value, scope, cost, and impact of the ideas, and approve those ideas that warrant advancement at that time. For approved projects, the analysts develop a project plan for the AUL/user services that outlines technical specifications, costs, a time line, the anticipated workload, potential challenges or barriers, other details and considerations, and a recommendation from among several options. The analysts may need to evaluate a technical or technological aspect of the project and coordinate with library or campus information technology units. Analysts may also need to consult with numerous individuals and groups across user services areas for projects that are likely to impact staff or users.

During the implementation process, feedback must be gathered and progress must be communicated. The analysts or others, such as a user services committee related to the project, may offer staff and users training and education. In some cases, marketing activities are required to alert users to the availability of a new service, tool, feature, resource, or facility. Following implementation, the analysts may compose a final report documenting the project, including challenges faced, benefits anticipated, and lessons learned. The analysts or others may perform subsequent monitoring to ensure that the project's goals were met and the implementation was successful. In some cases, assessments are subsequently conducted on an annual or otherwise iterative basis for continual project oversight and improvement.

Selected Projects of the Decision Support and User Services Technology Analysts

In recent years, changes and initiatives that have influenced the analysts' work have included the libraries' move toward greater self-service, the consolidation of selected service points and operational units, the creation of new study and computing spaces, collection reviews, and strategic planning. Additionally, the state of California's strained financial situation has significantly impacted the analysts' roles and projects. Issues and investigations to help the libraries accommodate the University of California's budget cuts dominated much of 2009, leaving limited time for researching or implementing new projects. Further budget issues arose in 2010 and 2011, and are likely to continue into the near future.

One of the decision support analyst's first tasks was to coordinate and implement the libraries' initial foray into usability testing. This was viewed as critical for successfully redesigning and maintaining the libraries' website. Results provided invaluable user insight which directly influenced the site's development. The analyst has since conducted a variety of usability tests on different parts of the libraries' website, examining components such as tab and heading names, terminology, formatting, functionality, and more. Each project has informed the continual modification and enhancement of the libraries' online presence. The analyst has also developed a long term usability plan for the libraries which documents the importance of conducting usability studies regularly and outlines a strategy for accomplishing this. This plan has further helped to solidify the libraries' commitment to its strategic planning initiatives by providing a framework for systematic and consistent usability testing.

As the decision support analyst has become recognized throughout the libraries as its usability and assessment expert, she has provided assistance and guidance to staff and committees assigned to evaluate the services for which they are responsible. Working with an individual or group to develop an assessment or evaluation plan, the analyst poses questions to elicit and understand the precise goals for the assessment. The analyst also assists individuals or groups with selecting an appropriate methodology, conducting the assessment or usability testing, and presenting the results. Recent projects have included usability testing of an introductory online tutorial for the libraries, usability testing involving the libraries' interface for its locally produced digital collections, and an assessment of the content of chat, text, and e-mail reference questions.

The decision support analyst is heavily involved in analysis of data for the libraries' space reconfiguration efforts, calculating seating capacities and fill rates for various spaces throughout the libraries' buildings to better understand where different amounts or types of seating might be needed. The analyst gathers and arranges existing raw data, organizes it, and presents it via the detailed annual seating inventory. This useful document directly contributes to administrators' thinking and planning regarding the use of space within library buildings, clarifying the types of library seating offered in each space and how the number and types of seating have changed over time. A photographic and observation study of new collaborative study spaces is currently in progress to understand how patrons adopt and use this space so that enhancements can be made to better serve user needs.

Other projects the decision support analyst has worked on to date include meeting informally with users, revising library and campus publications, compiling annual library statistics, inventorying existing statistics kept within the library in preparation of implementing the LibPAS statistical repository, reviewing proposals, participating in needs assessments, facilitating focus groups, conducting literature reviews and environmental scans, completing ARL SPEC surveys, conducting surveys with library users or library staff, analyzing the use of various electronic products to which the libraries subscribe, conducting wayfinding studies, revising and maintaining library signage, and reviewing and unifying the 4,000+ free-text notes in the online catalog. The analyst has conducted reviews of existing best practices policies and fees at other University of California and ARL libraries on such things as assessment activities, interlibrary loan charges and policies, reserves operations, digital information literacy initiatives, and organizational structure. She has also used gate counts, cost analyses, and other data to inform budget reduction strategies involving the use of service desks, library hours and staffing, and the consolidation of interlibrary loan units. The AUL/user services has used the decision support analyst's environmental scan of academic libraries experiences with LibQUAL in discussions with the university librarian about what types of assessment tools the libraries might consider using. Further, the analyst's review of Friends of the Library programs at other University of California campuses helped the AUL/user services and the libraries' director of development to consider additional services to provide to Friends members as a way to increase membership.

As lead for developing and comanaging projects involving library user services and IT, the user services technology analyst headed a cross-functional group that investigated how user services could be delivered effectively via mobile devices. This required an assessment and prioritization of which core library services are best suited for mobile access and an environmental scan of what similar institutions were already offering. The results informed the functional requirements for a mobile website. The analyst then led a small team of librarians and IT staff that worked collaboratively to draft the mobile site content while also codesigning the user interface. This group is now charged with periodically reviewing and creating new mobile content and services.

Responsible for assessing existing library technology services and providing the libraries' administration with concrete recommendations as to whether a service should be continued, modified, or discontinued, the user services technology analyst also recently assessed the libraries' online database recommendation service. Developed as an in-house project several years ago, this service was beginning to show its age and anecdotal evidence indicated it had outlived its usefulness. A proper data-driven analysis, however, was required to determine which features of the service were no longer necessary and which needed to be migrated to a newer technology. Working with library IT staff, the analyst collected extensive, multiyear usage data, which provided a clear indication that the vast majority of librarian-recommended databases and websites were no longer relevant or applicable for patrons. This served as a justification and guide for weeding these recommendation entries and creating a much smaller and more focused collection of licensed content. The features the libraries should migrate for the service were also identified and re-created in a new platform.

Other recent tasks completed by the user services technology analyst include creating specifications for implementing an online self-booking system for study rooms, developing comparisons between enterprise-level consortial borrowing software, creating an inventory of library classrooms and librarian needs for these classrooms, and managing the libraries' transition to an updated public computing model. The user services technology analyst has also worked with the decision support analyst to perform a detailed gap analysis of the libraries' local online catalog, as the entire University of California system moves to primary reliance on a shared catalog.

Benefits and Challenges of the Analyst Model

The UCSD Libraries has realized a number of benefits by creating the decision support and user services technology analyst positions. The most significant benefits include the establishment of a flexible and readily available staffing resource to work on projects as they arise, the ability to tackle projects not necessarily appropriate for any one position, and the ability to finish projects the libraries had previously wished to conduct, but lacked the resources to make a high priority. The benefits of having individuals dedicated to supplying insight and analysis and ensuring that administrators and others have solid and complete information for making sound decisions are also recognized. The AUL/user services has noted the value of the data the analysts have provided and its role in the effectiveness and efficiency of management within her portfolio of responsibilities.

Analysts can also save administrators' time, by freeing them from conducting needed research or investigations to support decision making. The data and insight they provide for the libraries also create opportunities for the analysts to serve as a bridge between library administrators and staff and between the libraries and its users. As the point persons to monitor technology applications or assessment activities, the analysts can help to initiate, track, and sustain service assessment over time or identify and investigate possible technological features, practices, policies, or applications that could be leveraged across the library organization. As designed, the analyst positions take advantage of a staff member's existing skill set, while also developing individuals specifically to suit the organization's current and future needs. The possibility of sharing the analysts' knowledge and expertise with others by distributing their research and supporting documentation among consortial or other partners is an additional benefit. Selected work of the UCSD Libraries' analysts is shared with librarians at other University of California libraries.

The individuals in the analyst positions have also realized a number of benefits. They primarily have the satisfaction of seeing their work provide a central justification for positive changes to services and infrastructure, as their roles allow for significant and direct contributions to the libraries. The analysts gain a broad perspective of how the libraries function internally and how they serve to support the goals of the wider campus community. At the same time, the analysts have the opportunity to engage in a variety of projects, employ analytical tools, and share perspectives from fields outside the library. Analysts also learn valuable skills that can be transferred to other libraries or even other service industries.

Considerations for Libraries Thinking of Implementing the Analyst Model

Libraries considering implementing an analyst model to address their assessment and decision-support needs should consider several questions. Logistical issues related to recruitment or reassignment include whether the library can hire an additional person to fill the newly created role, or if the library can develop an existing staff member with the right set of skills and attributes. If an internal candidate is identified, will this individual's salary be renegotiated after moving into the new role, or will the change be considered a financially lateral move? Will a designated internal candidate immediately assume an analyst role full-time, or gradually assume responsibilities? The analyst role has strikingly different responsibilities. Thus, a transition to this position may be particularly challenging and require flexibility from all involved. Further, will the analyst lose any responsibilities, such as supervising others, that may adversely affect his or her professional growth or future employment opportunities? To ensure that proper administrative and technical support is provided, where should the analyst's physical office location be? While proximity to administration or one's supervisor may be convenient, it is unlikely to be essential.

Reporting lines are another important consideration. Will the analysts be located within the user services portfolio, be more closely aligned with collections, or be associated with another area of the library? Will the analyst report to a single administrator or to the library's administrative team? While it may be easiest for an analyst to report to a single individual, even if tasks are proposed by or assigned by several others, distributing reporting relationships may be appropriate in some instances. How much independence will be afforded to the analyst, and how broad will the scope of the analyst's role be? The answer to this question may depend upon the library's organizational structure, as well as the working styles and capabilities of the analyst and the individuals to whom the analyst reports. How much weight will be placed on analyst recommendations? Will library administrators be willing to support analyst recommendations and change existing policies and practices based upon analyst input and data?

Questions related to workload and activities must also be considered. How much work is determined in advance for a new analyst? Administrators may be eager to assign a list of existing projects the library has not been able to accomplish due to lack of time or staff to the analyst. Will projects be specifically assigned to the analyst, or should he or she be proactive in identifying projects to pursue? Depending upon an internal candidate's existing skill set, questions of training should also be considered. Will any specialized training be required to supplement the candidate's existing skill set, and if so, is funding available to support this? To help analysts remain abreast of trends, innovations, and best practices, professional development opportunities from both within and outside of traditional library venues must be supported. Technical or professional skills, such as website usability or assessment, must either be brought to the position, or learned through targeted training and development activities.

Analysts must have the ability to analyze facts and statistics, synthesize and visualize data for understanding by others, and make recommendations. The ability to work within the limitations of a library's budget, policy, culture, or resources while identifying and advocating for improvements that are based on sound judgment or analysis is important. Additionally, analysts should be able to anticipate what information or analysis might be needed, both for known assignments and for possible future projects.

A strong focus on the library user and interest in recommending improvements based on identified staff and user needs is necessary, along with the ability to coordinate, motivate, and manage individuals who may not directly report to your position. Analysts must have the ability to prioritize, follow up, manage their time and workload, and lead projects and people. An understanding of and commitment to the library's mission, values, goals, and strategic directions is also essential to guide an analyst's work. While trust and respect for the analyst is required of the library administration, the analyst must be politically adept and discrete as he or she talks to and works with a wide variety of individuals throughout the organization. Credibility, integrity, and objectivity are also essential, along with strong interpersonal and communication skills.

Analysts must consciously make themselves visible and valuable to others within the library to illustrate the worth of their position and their skills. Because their role within the organization is new, it is important for an analyst to continually demonstrate and emphasize the unique benefits the position brings to the library. While it is imperative to establish and maintain positive working relationships with as many colleagues as possible to support existing and future projects, analysts must refrain from showing favoritism toward any library unit or individual, as neutrality may be needed for projects impacting multiple areas of the library.

The lack of similar roles within other academic libraries poses a challenge for the UCSD Libraries' analysts, limiting the pool of professionals from which they may learn and collaborate. The fact that future employers or external colleagues involved in the peer-review appraisal process might not understand the analyst role or its value to the library is a concern, despite a wealth of skills transferrable to positions both within and outside of the libraries. The AUL/user services understands this and diligently works to explain the analyst's role to others.

Conclusion

As libraries face increased pressure to justify their value to users and the resources needed to accomplish their mission, there is a heightened need for valuable qualitative insight and quantitative data to inform decision making. To address this, the UCSD Libraries has identified and reassigned staff to solicit, produce, analyze, summarize, and document information needed by library administrators. In the first several years of their new assignments, both the decision support analyst and the user services technology analyst have demonstrated the value of solid data to support decision making and comparisons, facilitated the completion of ongoing projects, and permitted the advancement of new initiatives. The analysts have provided the AUL/user services with information that has allowed her to evaluate issues or ideas prior to making critical public services-related decisions, or directing or allocating resources. The analysts have also helped the AUL/user services to identify projects or opportunities that should not be pursued, saving the library from making inappropriate or ineffective staff and resource investments.

A lack of staffing to investigate and implement new initiatives often means that potentially valuable innovations fall to the wayside so that existing services may be sustained. Analysts can further investigate ideas, lead implementation efforts, and coordinate others in advancing desired projects. Through conference attendance, professional readings, and interaction with colleagues at other institutions, analysts may identify new ideas for service additions, modifications, or enhancements; assessments; and emerging technologies and tools. Analysts can help inform library decisions to change, update, or even eliminate existing services. Libraries considering adopting an analyst model, however, must carefully consider an analyst's reporting relationships, potential projects, and overall role within the library's organizational structure.

NOTES

1. Attendance at the Library Assessment Conference has grown from approximately 250 at the inaugural event in 2006 to 350 in 2008, and 450 at the third and most recent event in 2010.
2. James Fish, Jennifer Rutner, and ZsuZsa Koltay, "Using Today's Numbers to Plan Tomorrow's Services: Effective User Services Assessment" (presentation at the ALA Annual Conference and Exhibition, New Orleans, June 26, 2011); ALA Committee on Research and Statistics, "Maybe It Has Already Been Done: Locating Existing Data for Planning, Assessment, and Advocacy" (presentation at the ALA Annual Conference and Exhibition, New Orleans, June 27, 2011).
3. In 2005 *Newsweek* and the *2006 Kaplan/Newsweek College Guide* named UC San Diego the "hottest" institution in the United States for students to study science. See UC San Diego Jacobs School of Engineering, "UCSD Named 'Hottest for Science' by *Newsweek Guide*," 2005, www.jacobsschool.ucsd.edu/news/news_releases/release.sfe?id=421.
4. Academic Impressions, "Strengthening the IT/Library Staff Partnership" (webcast, December 16, 2010); Academic Impressions, "Strategic Planning for Library-IT Collaboration" (webcast, February 3, 2010).

LAUREL ANN LITTRELL

Office of Library Planning
and Assessment, Kansas
State University Libraries

9

Kansas State University Libraries Office of Library Planning and Assessment

KANSAS STATE UNIVERSITY LIBRARIES ESTABLISHED ITS Office of Library Planning and Assessment in 2010, after realizing that assessment, data coordination, and scholarly communication were becoming increasingly significant. Serving a research institution with an enrollment of 23,800 students in over 250 undergraduate, 65 master's, and 45 doctoral programs, Kansas State University Libraries honors the university's land grant mission by making collections and services available to all citizens of Kansas. Customer service is a deeply ingrained value that is important to the libraries and the university as a whole.

This chapter outlines the process the libraries followed to establish the Office of Library Planning and Assessment. It provides a description of the structural reorganization that led to the office's creation and the duties of the four librarians assigned to planning and assessment. The goals of the office are outlined and several projects that have been completed or are in progress are described. The chapter then concludes by introducing the office's plans for the immediate future.

Reorganizing for the Twenty-First Century

Kansas State University Libraries overhauled its entire organizational structure in 2010 to reflect the goals of the twenty-first-century academic library. Previous attempts to incorporate activities related to assessment, copyright, and scholarly communication into regular librarian duties were not resulting in the quality of work administrators or librarians desired. The reorganization resulted in a network of new offices and departments, creating departments for Faculty and Graduate Services, Undergraduate and Community Services, and University Archives and Special Collections. Public service departments notably realigned with user groups rather than academic disciplines. The Offices of Library Planning and Assessment, Communications and Marketing, and Administrative and Information Technology Services were established to provide infrastructure to serve the needs of multiple departments. Other technical services and collections-related departments that resulted included Metadata and Preservation, Content Development and Acquisitions, and Scholarly Communications and Publishing.

With the libraries' reorganization, the need for strong assessment capacity has increased, especially as new offices and departments seek to establish their missions and learn the needs of their clientele. The decision to realign public service departments by user groups rather than academic discipline, while experimental, has been particularly difficult. To determine whether this arrangement is viable, assessment data methodologies must be applied and data collected. To determine whether other newly formed departments, such as Scholarly Communications and Publishing, are meeting the needs of the university and state and are performing as expected, additional user and needs assessments are required.

The Office of Library Planning and Assessment

Prior to the libraries' overhaul of its entire organizational structure, planning and assessment responsibilities were distributed among various department heads and administrators. As these responsibilities increased in significance in response to the changing environment over the years, it became clear that additional staff resources were needed. The libraries could only minimally comply with university assessment plan requirements and were unable to produce the quality of work expected. Annual reports to the university's Office of Assessment, for example, were brief and often included ideas for future implementation that the libraries could not realize. During the reorganization, the concept of an Office of Library Planning and Assessment emerged, envisioned as a small team of dedicated librarians with the ability to execute a number of group and individual projects.

Charged to assist the university and other library departments with planning, assessment, and accreditation activities, the office consists of four dedicated librarians, with well-defined roles: the director of library planning and assessment, the library data coordinator, the research and development librarian, and the service quality librarian. All positions except the service quality librarian were hired internally in July 2010. After an external recruitment, the service quality librarian was appointed in January 2011.

The director of library planning and assessment reports to the dean of libraries and participates in the libraries' Strategic Leadership Council. The director is responsible for providing leadership and vision for strategic planning, monitoring the plan's implementation, providing progress reports and updates, and ensuring that the libraries' strategic initiatives remain aligned with the university's strategic agenda. The director must develop a sustainable user-centered assessment program, focusing on student learning outcomes, library instruction, the integration of information literacy into the curriculum, reference and information services, collections and learning resources, collaborations with faculty and other academic staff, and the library as place. The director collaborates with leadership across the libraries and the university to foster a culture of assessment, working closely with administration and management teams to effectively engage and apply the information gathered in decision-making and planning processes. She is responsible for identifying, defining, and developing appropriate assessment approaches, measures, and techniques, as well as providing analysis of assessment-related data.

The director must develop, coordinate, promote, and communicate assessment activities and results to appropriate individuals and groups, including library staff and the campus community. In this capacity she works closely with staff responsible for public relations; web services; research, education, and engagement; content management and scholarly communications; and administration. The director evaluates the effectiveness of assessment activities to strengthen the libraries' assessment work and maintains awareness of the university's expectations for measurement and assessment. She supervises the three librarians assigned to the Office of Library Planning and Assessment and represents the libraries on campus assessment and planning groups. She also participates in national assessment activities and organizations.

The director must possess familiarity with library quantitative and qualitative assessment measures and analysis of results. Knowledge of academic libraries' work in research and development is also required, along with a demonstrated understanding of the development of library strategic goals and objectives. The capacity to thrive in an environment of change and foster this capacity in others is expected, and the director must possess excellent communication and organizational skills. The director must be able to work collaboratively with all levels of staff and model this behavior to others. She must also demonstrate a commitment to staff development and cross-departmental collaboration and communication, as well as a strong customer service orientation.

The library data coordinator is responsible for the timely collection of library statistics from various sources. This librarian must have an in-depth knowledge of library systems, associated library data structures, and library metadata attributes; understand library terminology; and understand the libraries' contextual need for various data and report. The data coordinator helps individuals maintaining data to provide useful information and to present data in meaningful ways. She is responsible for ensuring that data is compiled for reporting, planning and evaluation purposes and is disseminated properly. The data coordinator gathers monthly and annual library statistics from all individuals maintaining data, and coordinates the libraries' response to external requests for data from directories, membership surveys, institutional research surveys, and other higher-education surveys. The data coordinator identifies organizational structures and business models for successful data management, streamlines data collection and management processes, and maintains an authoritative data set for statistics and user feedback. She provides consulting services for statistical analysis, develops and offers training and technical assistance for selecting and using data collection tools, and generates reports upon request for library and university administration. The data coordinator also creates and maintains documentation related to data collection and assessment for the office.

The data coordinator must be detail-oriented and possess superior organizational skills. She must be familiar with statistical analysis and knowledgeable about library terminology and the types of reports generated by libraries. The data coordinator must understand the sources requesting library data and the purpose of this data, and possess a working knowledge of tools such as Microsoft Excel and Microsoft Access. She must have excellent oral and written communication skills, excellent interpersonal skills, and a strong service orientation. The data coordinator must also possess an ability and willingness to work with diverse groups, as well as colleagues in collaborative and team environments.

The research and development librarian works across departments to discover areas where new products, services, or practices could be developed, and determine whether and how existing products, services, and practices could be improved. The R&D librarian conceives of new ideas and determines their viability in relation to the libraries' strategic focus and future needs. Core position duties including conducting and applying research to the creation of new products, services, and practices; diffusing and adopting new products, services, and practices throughout the libraries that focus on internal process improvement or benefiting library customers directly; collaborating with campus units and other libraries; and identifying organizational structures and business models for successful research and development.

The R&D librarian must possess excellent analytical skills, knowledge of emerging services trends, and knowledge of emerging technologies in academic libraries. He must be familiar with research methodologies and be creative, innovative, and enjoy experimentation. This librarian must possess excellent communication and interpersonal skills, a strong service orientation, and an ability and willingness to work with diverse groups. An ability and willingness to work with colleagues in collaborative and team environments, as well as independently, is also required.

Last, the service quality librarian is responsible for gathering insights into customer expectations and satisfaction using a variety of assessment measures, and by actively engaging customers and monitoring the customer service experience. This librarian works across the libraries to develop a culture that values customer satisfaction and continuous improvement. The service quality librarian provides staff development and training, working closely with the Office of Public Relations, Marketing, and Communication. She collaborates with other units and departments, using ethnographic and other qualitative and quantitative methodologies to assess customer experiences.[1]

The service quality librarian is responsible for experimenting with new ideas and techniques to assess and improve the quality of customer service. This librarian also conducts user surveys, focus groups, and environmental scans, sharing results to improve customer experiences. In conjunction with university-wide and library initiatives, the service quality librarian assesses student learning outcomes, builds and maintains a body of knowledge on customer preferences, and coordinates the libraries' participation in national service quality and student learning assessments. She is also responsible for monitoring current trends, issues, and best practices in assessment methods.

The service quality librarian must possess an understanding of quantitative and qualitative assessment methodologies and how they are utilized in academic libraries. An ability to create and execute user surveys and focus groups, as well as perform environmental scans in an academic library setting, is also required. This librarian must have successful project management experience; an affinity and aptitude for acquiring new knowledge and skills; and an ability to inspire a shared vision. Like other individuals in the Office of Planning and Assessment, the service quality librarian must have excellent oral and written communication skills, a strong service orientation, and an ability and willingness to work with diverse groups, as well as colleagues, in collaborative and team environments.

Projects and Accomplishments

When the Office of Library Planning and Assessment was established, the director was already involved in the university's re-accreditation by the Higher Learning Commission. Several projects were assigned to the office by the dean of libraries in consultation with the director. Some projects were previously responsibilities of various administrators and department heads that were transferred to the office, such as producing the annual assessment report for the university's Office of Assessment, interfacing with the library instruction programs regarding student learning outcomes, or planning for the administration of LibQUAL. Additional guidance for the office was provided by the libraries' Strategic Leadership Council, a group comprised of administrators, department heads, and directors that meets on a weekly basis.

The implementation and prioritization of current projects are determined by a project's scope, timeliness, and urgency. Large university-level projects such as strategic planning, the university assessment reports, and accreditation take precedence over smaller, internally focused projects. Projects are assigned to office librarians based upon a project's relevance to individual positions as well as current workloads and upcoming deadlines for other projects. Since many librarians outside the office have expertise in planning and assessment areas, they are encouraged to continue to use and build those skills on the library departmental level. Librarians in the office provide feedback, perspective, and context for assessment- and planning-related projects outside of the office by serving as advisory members of committees and task forces. Recent projects involving the Office of Library Planning and Assessment that have been completed or have seen considerable progress include the university's re-accreditation; developing the libraries' strategic plan; assisting with usability testing for website review; developing an assessment plan for student learning outcomes; conducting an internal staff assessment of the recent reorganization; and assisting the newly formed departments with assessing the needs of their user groups.

The Higher Learning Commission visited Kansas State University in April 2012 for the university's re-accreditation site visit. To support the re-accreditation, the director of the Office of Library Planning and Assessment contributed information and data about the libraries, chaired a committee gathering information for one of the self-study chapters, and drafted parts of two other self-study chapters. In addition, the office hosted the Resource Room for the site visit team in the main library and provided assistance in organizing and filing hundreds of documents. These documents were indexed, cross-referenced, and provided to the site visit team in an electronic format.

As the central administration launched a new university-wide strategic plan in the fall of 2011, the Office of Library and Planning and Assessment has been closely following the university's new strategic planning process, known as K-State 2025. The office has participated in the K-State 2025 meetings, kept library colleagues informed of the status of the process, and offered feedback on drafts of the university-wide plan. In 2012, each area of the university must begin developing new strategic plans that demonstrate how all the colleges and operating units will contribute to the overall university plan. The Office of Library Planning and Assessment will be leading and coordinating the libraries' planning process, gathering and compiling data, providing guidance and assistance to task forces developing the plan, and providing university officials with progress reports. The university strategic plan emphasizes increasing research activity for all faculty and students, especially undergraduates. This will significantly impact the library and its ability to support research. The university's attention to research is not limited to the sciences or social sciences, but includes scholarship and creative activities for all academic areas. For librarians, this emphasis in the university's strategic plan not only provides opportunities to support faculty and students' research, but for librarians to perform research and creative activities themselves, either on their own or in collaboration with other librarians or faculty members. The Office of Library Planning and Assessment is prepared to offer librarians support, data, and advice in conducting research and developing new services.

The libraries' last strategic plan culminated in 2012 with the extensive reorganization that created the Office of Library Planning and Assessment and other new departments. A final report summarizing this plan was generated by the Office of Library Planning and Assessment to provide closure and launch the new library strategic plan. Formulating and implementing the new strategic plan will be a continuing high priority in the coming months and years.

LibQUAL Lite was launched in the spring of 2011 under the leadership of the service quality librarian. Measurable improvements in the survey's "library as place" and "affect of service" categories reflect changes made following the libraries' 2007 participation in LibQUAL. These changes include the addition of a number of group study areas within the main library, an increase in available seating and desktop computers throughout the libraries, and a relaxation of food and beverage policies. Several service points were consolidated since 2007 to alleviate confusion for where to request assistance. Library hours also were increased, and building navigation was improved with maps, signs, and guides. The results indicated that more attention must be given to the needs of graduate students and faculty, further reinforcing the establishment of the Faculty and Graduate Services Department to emphasize the needs of these groups. Access to online information and the usability of the library website were also identified as needing improvement.

The service quality librarian prepared reports of the LibQUAL results which included both the quantitative and qualitative data. These results were communicated to the university community through a number of venues, including the Faculty Senate Library Committee and a campuswide presentation as part of a university assessment conference. Results will be presented to the university's undergraduate and graduate student councils. A website is in development to track progress on projects identified following analysis of the survey results. Recommendations for further investigation of problem areas are also in development.

While the 2011 LibQUAL data indicated ongoing dissatisfaction with the library website, a complete website overhaul was already in progress as part of the libraries' reorganization. The service quality librarian participated in developing usability testing for the newly reconfigured library website to determine specific areas for improvement. This testing proved highly valuable and provided much insight to the team responsible for developing the site. As development work continues, usability testing will proceed to improve access and ease of use.

To develop the annual reports required by the university Office of Assessment, the libraries' assessment office formed a committee of representatives from departments providing instruction, reference, and collection development services. In contrast to previous reports which noted many deficiencies, recent reports have received favorable reviews. The formulation of the Office of Library Planning and Assessment, with staff devoted to compiling data and creating these reports, has directly influenced the report's quality. The libraries have been further able to demonstrate their value and place in the academic endeavors of the university by providing much more useful information. This is especially significant as the university is now interested in increasing the participation of cocurricular areas such as the libraries in assessment activities to demonstrate the contributions of these areas to student learning and success. While most of the libraries' student learning assessments to date have been in partnership with degree programs, it is the desire of both the Office of Library Planning and Assessment and the university Office of Assessment to see the library begin to create independent student learning assessment activities. The results of these assessments will help determine how the libraries may contribute to the learning environment, improve services, and ultimately enhance the outcome of students' study at Kansas State University.

Other projects developed and implemented by the Office of Library Planning and Assessment include a Staff Reorganization Survey, which was conducted in October and November 2011. The libraries desired to evaluate the reorganization from the perspective of library faculty and staff. The survey surfaced many useful ideas for improvement to the new organizational structure for consideration. Comments provided observations about where workflow problems could be improved, identified areas experiencing staff shortages, provided suggestions for improvement in communication, identified areas where additional training was needed, and revealed a desire to learn more about the work of others within the library. With most of the faculty and staff in the library changing positions and performing different duties, it has taken more than a year for individuals to learn their new jobs, receive available training, and become accustomed to their new roles and routines. As people become assimilated into their new operating units and departments, the next phase of the reorganization is for individuals to become familiar with other departments, to provide greater context for their own work and how it interacts and contributes to the libraries' overall mission.

Lastly, the research and development librarian has been studying a number of new ideas for potential implementation. One project he is currently working on with other public services librarians involves using QR Codes to assist faculty and students in locating resources and facilitating building or campus navigation. Another project is the establishment of an undergraduate diversity internship. These internships are intended to provide opportunities for students to seek part-time employment to work on projects within the library, with the goal of furthering the libraries' and the university's mission to enrich the diversity climate on campus, enhance the undergraduate research experience, and introduce librarianship as a potential career choice. They also contribute to the university's strategic goal of creating more research opportunities for undergraduate students.

Finally, the R&D librarian is exploring ideas pertaining to embedded librarianship, especially as applied to online or distance education courses, to provide assistance and encourage students to seek the assistance of librarians on their projects and assignments. The concepts surfaced by the R&D librarian for this initiative have been readily adapted by librarians participating in instruction and successfully incorporated into several classes.

Looking to the Future

The Office of Library Planning and Assessment has ambitious goals for the future, with the development and implementation of a new strategic plan as a centerpiece. Other significant goals include developing a culture of assessment, improving student learning outcomes assessment, and pursuing research and development projects.

With the implementation of K-State 2025, the libraries' new strategic plan must define how it will contribute to the university's goals and identify the resources the libraries requires to accomplish its goals. Availability of accurate, easy-to-access information from assessment efforts and established data-gathering methods will inform decisions and aid the task forces and individuals developing this plan. Supporting the university's increased research mission, particularly for undergraduate students, will provide the library additional opportunities to offer service and outreach in new and different ways.

A culture of assessment is developing within the libraries. By regularly using tools such as LibQUAL, in concert with locally developed assessment methods, we are further refining services, collections, and our libraries' virtual and physical environments. By continuing to improve our assessment methods for student learning outcomes, we will also be able to enhance the libraries' impact on the learning environment. Proposed projects include assessing the learning of students who work in the library to determine if there is any correlation between their employment, increased exposure to library resources, and their academic experiences. Other project ideas include an ethnographic study of students, faculty, and staff who do not use library resources on a regular basis. Questions to answer include whether there are academic disciplines with fewer resource needs than others, or whether students and faculty are locating information elsewhere because they are unaware of the information that is already available to them via the libraries. Academic libraries in general have wrestled with these questions for many years and are continuing to ask them in efforts to increase awareness and improve services.

The research and development librarian, in collaboration with others, will continue to monitor trends and developments, investigate new ideas for potential application, and facilitate projects. Future project ideas include maximizing the usefulness of mobile devices, as student use of tablets and smart phones continues to increase. Access to information through these smaller devices requires a completely different format and delivery, requiring libraries to transition away from web pages to interfaces that will be readable and navigable on small screens. Such interfaces must also deliver the quality and quantity of information required for collegiate study. By observing other libraries' efforts in this area, the Office of Library Planning and Assessment can optimize these new tools without duplicating efforts. In addition to the technology-related projects mentioned, plans are in place to examine and streamline other services and components of library work, through projects related to human resources processes and providing students with more research opportunities.

Conclusion

By establishing the Office of Library Planning and Assessment and staffing it with a director and three librarians, Kansas State University Libraries has developed a comprehensive, thorough approach to assessment and planning that is already yielding positive results. Data collection and organization have improved and assessment plans and reports are more fully developed.

Further, the office has facilitated the exploration of new technologies and services, and increased the use of existing library and university assessment data. The libraries' considerable involvement in the Higher Learning Commission accreditation visit, and its capacity to fulfill the university's strategic planning expectations will increase the libraries' visibility to the campus community. The Office of Library Planning and Assessment has established its credibility with other library departments as well as the university, and can now leverage this credibility for the good of the library and the university as a whole.

NOTE

1. Nancy Fried Foster and Susan Gibbons, *Studying Students: The Undergraduate Research Project at the University of Rochester* (Chicago: Association of College and Research Libraries, 2007).

LUCRETIA MCCULLEY

Boatwright Memorial Library,
University of Richmond, Virginia

10

Building an Assessment Program in the Liberal Arts College Library

NOW IN ITS FOURTH YEAR, THE LIBRARY ASSESSMENT COMMITtee at the University of Richmond has made great strides in establishing a sustainable assessment program within Boatwright Library. Prior to 2008, limited staff, time, expertise, and commitment were barriers to establishing an ongoing assessment program.[1] As with many other liberal arts college libraries, most of our assessment efforts had focused on information literacy, since instruction is integral to the library and the university's mission. Library surveys and other assessment methods had only received close attention when the university was embarking on its re-accreditation process. With the growing emphasis on assessment within higher education and the emergence of a new strategic plan for the university, the university librarian made a commitment to build a formal library assessment program.[2] Jim Self and Steve Hiller, Association of Research Libraries consultants, visited the University of Richmond in the fall of 2008 to offer the "Effective, Sustainable and Practical Library Assessment" analysis, their first visit at a small liberal arts institution.[3]

Librarians at liberal arts college libraries perform multiple duties, and it is rare to find a library staff member totally dedicated to assessment and trained in statistical analysis at such institutions.[4] Our goals for the Hiller-Self visit were to identify strategies and ideas that might work and prove sustainable in our unique institution. As a result of that visit, the library formed an assessment committee, composed of five individuals representing various departments of the library. Since that time, the committee has made numerous advances in building a culture of assessment in the library. This chapter will describe one model of creating an assessment program in a liberal arts college setting.

Institutional Context

The University of Richmond is a private, highly selective, nationally ranked liberal arts university. Located in Virginia's capital city, the University of Richmond offers the atmosphere of a small college with strong academic, research, and cultural opportunities. It also provides a unique combination of undergraduate and graduate programs through its schools of arts and sciences, business, leadership studies, law, and continuing studies. The institution has an enrollment of 3,900 students and offers 60 undergraduate majors and a small number of graduate programs (i.e., MBA, Law, and School of Continuing Studies). Over 350 full-time faculty members teach at the university, and the average student faculty ratio is 8:1.

Boatwright Memorial Library's mission is "to provide University of Richmond students, faculty, and staff with information resources and services that enable them to excel in their academic and intellectual pursuits." The library includes major collections in the sciences, fine arts, music, humanities, social sciences, film, maps, theater, government documents, and rare books and manuscripts. At present, there are over a half a million volumes of books, more than 30,000 electronic and print periodicals, and thousands of multimedia items in the collection. Numerous electronic resources are available through the library and the college's computer labs, as well as from outside the library through the library's website. The library is an extremely popular destination on campus, serving as a social, study, and cultural center, and had over 557,000 visits in 2010–2011. In 2010 the library created a five-year strategic plan, focusing on "creating inspiring space for student, staff and faculty; providing resources to promote learning; and emphasizing communication and education to accelerate innovation and discovery."[5]

Creating a Library Assessment Committee

The Library Assessment Committee has provided the primary impetus and enthusiasm for establishing a culture of assessment within Boatwright Library. Chaired by the director of outreach services, the committee consists of five members who represent a variety of positions and departments within the library. Our first task as a committee in 2008 was to establish the committee's charge and assessment goals. (See figure 10.1.)

In addition to creating our charge and developing goals, we also devoted time to educating ourselves about library assessment. Steve Hiller and Jim Self had provided numerous readings, reports, and websites during their visit and we followed up on many of their recommendations. We also read other books and articles on the subject and shared our collective knowledge on assessment among the group. In those first few months of the committee's existence, we focused on the assessment data that the library had readily available, such as annual statistics, reports from an internal "think team" process, and faculty/student interviews conducted by liaison librarians. Reviewing and analyzing the existing data gave the group a sense of focus and purpose, in addition to helping the group solidify its working relationship.

Another early priority of the committee was to educate and inform the staff on what assessment means to them, the library organization, and the institution. Many staff felt threatened by the term and thought it meant that they would be constantly evaluated. We tried to alleviate these fears by sharing minutes of our meetings; sending out informative e-mails to the entire staff; and holding all-staff assessment forums. During that first year, we were also instrumental in establishing a goals process for the library and worked with an organizational consultant to plan an annual retreat, focusing on the revision of the library's annual goals and the creation of a vision statement for the library. As the months passed, all of these components came together with the creation of an assessment plan to guide our work within the library.[6] The plan includes the library's mission statement, vision statement, annual library

FIGURE 10.1
Library Assessment Committee Charge and Goals

Committee Charge

The Library Assessment Committee is responsible for coordinating and providing oversight of various assessment activities in Boatwright Memorial Library; educating staff on library assessment; publishing and promoting assessment results; collaborating with the Office of Institutional Effectiveness; and promoting a culture of assessment that is user-focused.

Committee Goals
- To respond to the needs of our users.
- To maintain and improve our programs, collections, and services.
- To assist all library staff in "taking action" to monitor and improve services.
- To assist staff in using data, not assumptions, to make decisions.
- To identify library services that relate to the library goals and the university's strategic plan.

---

goals, and the committee's charge as well as assessment goals and priorities for each year. The plan is updated on an annual basis.

A high priority for the committee was to design and create a library assessment web page, in order to promote our assessment efforts to the library staff, provide transparency of assessment data, and share our progress with the university community.[7] This resource has become an important component of our emphasis on assessment for both the library and the university. Our vision was to create an assessment page that was more than statistics and numbers, and offered colorful and interesting graphics to appeal to viewers. After reviewing numerous assessment web pages at other academic and public libraries, we decided on a design that would highlight specific statistics with rotating graphics and that would then link out to detailed statistics. We also post SACS (Southern Association of Colleges and Schools) assessment plans, reports and studies on various surveys and interviews, and other pertinent assessment information. The web page provides a central place for library staff, the university community, and other libraries to discover our assessment efforts and statistical data.

Collaboration with the Office of Institutional Effectiveness (OIE) at the University of Richmond has been an important component of our assessment program. Assessment specialists from OIE have met with the director of outreach services frequently, offering advice and guidance through the annual SACS assessment plans and reports. The OIE staff members have enthusiastically endorsed the library's interest in assessment and they often refer to us as a model unit on campus.

Continuing education has also played an important role in the establishment of our program. The director of outreach services has attended all of the ARL Assessment Conferences (2006, 2008, 2010), in addition to special programs and workshops on assessment at ALA and ARCL conferences. In 2009 she attended the Immersion Conference on Assessment and Information Literacy, sponsored by the ACRL. The social sciences and humanities librarian on the assessment committee also attended the 2010 Assessment Conference, and both librarians made presentations at this conference. The stacks, building, and interlibrary loan supervisor attended a Council on Library and Information Resources workshop on ethnographic methods in the spring of 2011. The entire committee takes advantage of webinars, books, journal articles, blog postings, and other opportunities to increase our knowledge of assessment.

Assessment Tools and Methods

Since the fall of 2008, the committee has initiated several assessment projects, both large and small. Assessment tools have varied, but in these first three years, we have primarily relied on survey methods. Without a statistician on the library staff, we were creative in identifying options for surveys that offer built-in analyses and results. For example, in the last three years the library was involved in utilizing three national survey packages, the Counting Opinions LIBSAT Survey, the HEDS/NITLE Research Practices Survey, and the MISO (Measuring Information Service Outcomes) Survey.[8] Small-scale surveys for various specific library services, such as course reserves, document delivery, and library space issues, have been accomplished using Student-Voice/CampusLabs, a survey software provided by the Student Development Division at the University of Richmond. StudentVoice/CampusLabs is a user-friendly survey system that combines elements of data collection, reporting, organization, and integration. In addition, assessment specialists at Student-Voice/CampusLabs are available for consultation and review of surveys. The service is in the process of changing its name to CampusLabs to emphasize its broader commitment and focus to assessment. Not only does it offer survey software and analysis, but tools for assessing learning, including rubric creation, are available on the website. Other tools include Project Dashboard, which provides appealing graphics on statistics, survey results, and studies that can be used on a web page or inserted into a document.

In addition to online surveys, some library departments have found value in using brief print surveys to obtain user feedback on specific services, such as netbook circulation in the library. The library's main service desk has circulated laptops to students within the building for many years and when there was a need for an equipment upgrade, we chose to purchase netbooks, rather than laptops. In order to gauge student satisfaction/dissatisfaction with this change, the staff asked students to fill out a brief paper survey after each checkout session. This method offered a quick way to obtain user feedback on an important student service.

Other assessment tools include observation studies and the continued analysis of library statistical data. For example, the library's electronic resources librarian regularly uses database and journal use statistics to assist liaison librarians in making decisions about canceling print journal subscriptions, or ordering new electronic journals. Library Systems staff regularly share data on library catalog use and circulation statistics.

One of the most exciting recent developments of the Library Assessment Committee has been the establishment of a three-person ethnographic team in the library. This development is the perfect example of establishing a culture of assessment in the library. Not only is the Library Assessment Committee keenly interested in assessment, but we now have other staff members who are committed to the program. One member of the ethnographic team serves on the Assessment Committee for coordination and communication purposes. The team has been instrumental in establishing observation studies in the library, and they have formed an excellent collaboration with a professor in the university's Sociology and Anthropology Department who is interested in studying library culture. During the spring of 2011, the team worked closely with an anthropology student who designed focus groups to receive feedback on the library building. During the fall of 2011, the team worked with the professor and her entire anthropological field methods class to study student behavior in the library. This is an excellent example of collaborating with others on campus to increase our knowledge, but to also take advantage of expertise that we do not have among the library staff. Similar to the above-mentioned statistician example, we could not afford to hire a full-time anthropologist, but we are making the most of the resources that we do have available to us.

Assessment Findings

Boatwright Library's areas of assessment emphasis include student learning, user services, and building facilities. Student learning assessment strategies in the past two years focused on data collected through the HEDS/NITLE Research Practices Survey. Currently, we are focused on assessing the information literacy goals of the university's new First Year Seminars, where library workshops are required of each first-year student. We collaborate with faculty in assessing the information literacy component of the First Year Seminars with the use of a rubric tool. Librarians are also receiving usage statistics for newly created LIBGUIDES and feedback on the effectiveness of course-specific LIBGUIDES from brief in-class surveys asking students how they used the LIBGUIDE to prepare papers and projects.[9] To assess user services, over the past three years we have used the Counting Opinions LIBSAT Survey, the MISO Survey, and focused StudentVoice/CampusLabs surveys. To assess building facilities a variety of methods have been used, including observation studies, data extracted from the Counting Opinions and MISO Surveys, and feedback collected from the library's suggestion box.

How have we used the above assessment tools and how have our findings made a difference in our library services and sources? While thorough, detailed analysis of all our results cannot be shared in this chapter, I would like to share representative examples of our various tools, including a description of the tool, why we chose it, what we learned, and practical implications.

Counting Opinions LIBSAT Survey

Counting Opinions LIBSAT Survey is an instantaneous, continuous customer feedback system that enables libraries to measure customer satisfaction and the impacts and outcomes of various endeavors over time. We have used the Counting Opinions LIBSAT Survey for the past two years to obtain ratings and comments from students, staff, and faculty at the university. We chose

Counting Opinions because we wanted to use a national survey package that would give us feedback on overall customer service satisfaction, easily compile results, and offer the opportunity to compare our library against similar libraries. Many libraries across the United States and Canada use the software, and support for implementation has been excellent. After viewing various demonstrations of Counting Opinions at conferences and through webinars, we decided to move forward with using the survey for three years. Counting Opinions also acts as a continuous feedback survey, since it is on our website for most of the academic year.

The Counting Opinions LIBSAT Survey was available on the library's website from October through April for both the 2009–2010 and 2010–2011 academic years. Targeted e-mail messages were sent throughout the year, reminding students, staff, and faculty to complete the survey. In the first year, 191 users responded to the survey; 57 percent of respondents were undergraduates and 31 percent were faculty/staff. The remaining numbers included graduate students, alumni, visitors, and other students. Our goal for 2010–2011 was to increase our response rate, so we advertised more specifically to our major user groups (faculty, staff, and students) and we offered a gift certificate to a local café as an incentive. We nearly doubled our response rate with 404 responses (68 percent were undergraduates and 20 percent were faculty/staff).

Results from both years were very similar. Many questions in the Counting Opinions survey asked participants to rank their answers on a scale of 1 to 7. A rank of 7 means "strongly agree," a rank of 6 means "agree," and a rank of 5 means "somewhat agree." Other questions focused on satisfaction with and importance of various services, and those responses are also on a 7-point scale (Very Satisfied [7] to Very Dissatisfied [1] or Very Important [7] to Very Unimportant [1]). Overall results indicated that Boatwright Library is viewed favorably by faculty, staff and students. (See figures 10.2, 10.3.)

FIGURE 10.2

Counting Opinions LIBSAT Survey—Overall Results

Statement	Satisfaction/Agreement	
	2009–2010	*2010–2011*
Overall impressions I will reuse the services of this library.	6.0	6.0
This library is very important to me.	5.9	6.0
I will recommend the services of this library to others.	5.9	5.7
The quality of library services is very high.	5.7	5.7
I am very satisfied with the services of this library.	5.7	5.6
The services of this library consistently meet or exceed my expectations.	5.6	5.5

FIGURE 10.3

2010-2011 Counting Opinions LIBSAT Survey—Overall Results by Patron Type

Statement	Satisfaction/Agreement		
	Undergraduate	Graduate	Faculty/Staff
Overall impressions I will reuse the services of this library.	6.0	6.2	6.3
This library is very important to me.	5.9	5.7	6.1
I will recommend the services of this library to others.	5.9	6.2	6.1
The quality of library services is very high.	5.5	5.8	5.9
I am very satisfied with the services of this library.	5.7	5.8	5.9
The services of this library consistently meet or exceed my expectations.	5.6	5.8	5.9

The Counting Opinions LIBSAT Survey provided feedback that our services are ranked highly and they are appreciated by the university community. The survey results also highlighted areas for improvement, especially with our physical facility and the need to add more study space, additional tables, and computers. We used the feedback to share evidence of users' requests for additional and improved space. For example, many users were concerned about restrooms in the library, and University Facilities has now planned future improvements for that space. During the summer of 2010, the Library Assessment Committee gathered comments and ratings from Counting Opinions on physical space and combined it with our observation studies and other data to create a focused report on physical and environmental needs in Boatwright Library.[10]

Document Delivery Satisfaction Survey

Document Delivery provides delivery of books, articles, and reference book chapters for items that Boatwright Library owns in print format to all faculty and staff. Articles are scanned and sent to faculty and staff via e-mail, while books are delivered on campus to departments. The Document Delivery service is a cooperative effort between two library services, Interlibrary Loan

(ILL) and the Media Resource Center (MRC), and makes use of both full-time and student employees. During the 2008–2009 academic year, the library chose to assess the Document Delivery service as one of the outcomes for the SACS Assessment Plan. To evaluate the service, ILL and MRC staff tracked the number of books processed for document delivery and the number of books delivered within two working days. A short, two-question survey was also developed using the StudentVoice/CampusLabs Survey software. The first question focused on delivery time to offices and the second question asked about their overall satisfaction with the service. A section for comments was also provided.

The Document Delivery service is very popular on campus, but we wanted to make sure faculty were receiving materials when promised and if there were any suggestions that would improve the service. It also gave us the chance to initiate the first use of the StudentVoice/CampusLabs survey tool on a small scale, since the survey would only be taken by faculty and staff that had used the service.

The statistics collected by ILL and MRC staff revealed that between January and April of 2009 over 1,000 books were delivered to faculty and staff. Of the books delivered, 99 percent were delivered within two business days. This was significantly higher than the predicted target of 80 percent and validated the efficiency of the service. The StudentVoice/CampusLabs survey data closely matched the data collected by ILL and the MRC. It was e-mailed to all users of the service and responses were anonymous. Results revealed that 88 percent of items were delivered within two business days, well above the target of 80 percent.[11]

We found that although users were very satisfied with our Document Delivery service, they did not fully understand various aspects of the service, such as why library staff could not deliver more than five items per day, or why items could not be picked up from office departments. They also lacked understanding on how to search for DVDs in the library catalog, and indicated they were dissatisfied with the online form for both interlibrary loan and document delivery. We chose to respond to all survey respondents and provide clarification on the above issues. The faculty comments about the online form helped interlibrary loan staff explore other options, such as ILLIAD software, for the service's interface.

We were very pleased with the use and performance of the StudentVoice/CampusLabs Survey software. It was easy to create a survey and distribute it to a specific population. Assessment specialists advised us on question wording and provided excellent support in using the system. We were pleased with the automatic gathering of data and the reports, both text and graphic, that the software provided for us.

Quiet and Group Study Observations and Survey

Boatwright Library is a popular place on campus, and students often complain that more study space, both quiet and group, is needed. As another outcome measure for the library's 2009–2010 SACS assessment plan, the Assessment Committee decided to gather information on quiet and group study area use using observation studies and a StudentVoice/CampusLabs Survey. Facility use is often difficult to measure and we felt that the combination of two methods, an observation study and a student survey, would offer different perspectives, but it would also offer a chance to compare the data to identify common or different trends. This method was also our first effort with observation studies, and its small-scale focus was an excellent way to begin learning more about observational methods.

The observation study took place during the 2009–2010 academic year at Boatwright Library. The observers (library staff and student library assistants) noted user behavior in the quiet and collaborative areas of the library using a standard form. The primary question to be answered was "Are users using group and quiet spaces as intended?" Observers recorded key information such as locations, day, time, and number of patrons on the form. They also were free to record observations from their perspective. Observations generally ranged in time from five minutes to a half hour depending on activity in the observation area.

Results revealed that quiet and group study areas were being used for the intended purpose 80 percent of the time. The study noted several other trends, such as users' tendency to carry a lot of items with them. These items include multiple bags, purses, food, multiple forms of technology, and books and notebooks for class work. Most of the time, the items were crowded around a library user, limiting the useable work space for them and occasionally their classmates at a shared table.

The StudentVoice/CampusLabs survey had a very high response rate of over 600 responses. Although most students were satisfied with the quiet and group study areas, the satisfaction rates are not as high as we would like. The survey comments were valuable in helping us identify the need for more tables and more space.

Results from the quiet and group observations and survey, combined with information from other sources, assisted us in writing a complete report on user comments and opinions about user space. This report is proving to be very helpful to library administrators as they find a solution to crowded stacks and crowded user space.[12] In October 2011 we learned that the university has awarded the library $2.5 million for a partial renovation on two floors of the library. We hope this renovation will provide the additional group study and quiet study areas that students requested.

First Year Seminar Information Literacy Assessment Rubric

As mentioned earlier, liaison librarians collaborated closely with faculty on the development of new First Year Seminars (FYS) during the summer of 2010. Information literacy is one of the five major goals of the program, and each seminar class has a librarian embedded within the course to teach and support information literacy assignments. We worked closely with staff in the Office of Institutional Effectiveness and the FYS Faculty Committee to create a rubric for faculty members to use in assessing information literacy. Although not perfect, feedback on the rubric has provided preliminary data that we can use to follow up with faculty and perhaps develop a more specific assessment in the future.

The stated outcome for the assessment rubric was "First Year Seminar students will be able to effectively access and utilize information from a variety of sources." Students' achievement of this outcome was assessed by using a writing assignment selected by the instructor during the spring semester seminars and applying the standardized rubric. The assessment goal was that 70 percent of students would be rated as "meets expectations" or "exceeds expectations" for each criterion on the rubric. The target for this assessment was met, with 70 percent of students rated as "meets expectations" or "exceeds expectations" for each criterion on the rubric. (See figure 10.4.)

FIGURE 10.4

Information Literacy Rubric Assessment Results

Rubric Rating	Exceeds Expectations	Meets Expectations	Fails to Meet Expectations
Determine the extent of information needed	32% (241/762)	57% (438/762)	11% (83/762)
Access the needed information effectively and efficiently	32% (246/777)	60% (467/777)	8% (64/777)
Evaluate information and its sources critically	28% (213/762)	58% (442/762)	14% (107/762)
Use information effectively to accomplish a specific purpose	32% (252/778)	57% (447/778)	10% (79/778)
Access and use information ethically and legally	32% (251/777)	62% (484/777)	5% (42/777)

Library Statistics

Gathering and sharing pertinent library statistics has been of interest at Boat-wright Library. While collection statistics are important, they do not hold the emphasis that they might in a research library institution. We are more interested in "telling our story" with our service statistics, that is, how many research consultations we have provided for students, how many full-text journals, how many uses of our website, or how many times our group study room was checked out. We constantly ask ourselves how our statistics and assessment data can show our value to the community. Recently, we brought together several staff and librarians together for conversations focusing on such questions as (1) what statistics do we need for national surveys, such as the ACRL's Academic Libraries Trends and Statistics Survey? (2) what information do we need for internal decision making? and (3) what data do we need to tell our value to the campus community?[13]

Conclusion

Assessment can be accomplished in a small liberal arts institution with support from the library director, commitment to assessment at the university level, and motivation and desire among the library staff. Boatwright Library's successes in the past three years have shown that persistent and focused activities have resulted in a sustainable program. However, it is important to recognize that implementing an effective program must be taken in small steps, using the staff time that is realistically available. Staff interest and appreciation of how assessment can help librarians understand our users' perspectives have benefited the library staff, both internally and externally. Boatwright's Assessment Committee is enthusiastic, energetic, and committed. The assessment web page has enabled the library to share key assessment data with the larger community. We have also created a regular electronic newsletter and a digital annual report, which provide further ways to tell the library's story and value.

The committee's focus is changing as we have become confident with how assessment fits into our organization and with our goals. Our first year focused on how to form a committee or how to write an assessment plan, and the group met twice a month in order to establish a ground level of functionality. As we complete three years as a committee, we are spending more time on analyzing data and developing methods supporting more "hands on" assessment with other library staff. We have also noticed that various staff members around the library are embarking on their own assessment projects. Slowly but surely, a culture of assessment is taking root in our environment.

NOTES

1. Harvey Varnet and Martha Rice Sanders, "Asking Better Questions: Small-Scale Assessment Measures That Inform Ongoing Work," *College and Research Libraries News* 66, no. 6 (2005): 461.
2. University of Richmond, "The Richmond Promise: A Strategic Plan for the University of Richmond, 2009–2014," https://strategicplan.richmond.edu/.
3. Association of Research Libraries, Statistics and Assessment, "Effective, Sustainable and Practical Assessment," www.arl.org/stats/initiatives/esp/.
4. Delores Skowronek and Larry Duerr, "The Convenience of Nonprobability: Survey Strategies for Small Academic Libraries," *College and Research Libraries News* 70, no. 7 (2009): 415.
5. Boatwright Memorial Library, University of Richmond, "Boatwright Memorial Library Strategic Plan, 2010-2011," May 2010, http://library.richmond.edu/about/library-assessment.html.
6. Boatwright Memorial Library, University of Richmond, "Assessment Plan for Boatwright Memorial Library," 2009, http://library.richmond.edu/documents/library-assessment-plan.pdf.
7. Boatwright Memorial Library, "Library Assessment Webpage," http://library.richmond.edu/about/library-assessment.html.
8. Counting Opinions: Solutions for Libraries, "Counting Opinions LIBSAT Survey," www.countingopinions.com; National Institute for Technology in Liberal Education, "Research Practices Survey," www.nitle.org/casestudies/improving_student_info_literacy.php; MISO: Measuring Information Service Outcomes, www.misosurvey.org.
9. Springshare, "LIBGUIDES," www.springshare.com/libguides/features.html.
10. Travis Smith, "Where We Stand (and Sit): Quiet and Group Study Space Use at Boatwright Library," 2010, http://library.richmond.edu/documents/Quiet-Group-Study-Report.pdf.
11. Boatwright Memorial Library, University of Richmond, "Document Delivery Survey Final Report," 2009, http://library.richmond.edu/documents/Document%20Delivery%20Survey%20Final%20Report.pdf.
12. Lucretia McCulley and Travis Smith, "'Library as Place': User Feedback and Opinions on Boatwright Library's Building Facility," 2010, http://library.richmond.edu/documents/Library%20as%20Place%20Report.pdf.
13. Association of College and Research Libraries, Academic Library Statistics, "Academic Library Trends and Statistics Survey," www.ala.org/acrl/publications/trends.

CAROL MOLLMAN

Washington University in St. Louis

11

Developing a Library Assessment Program at Washington University in St. Louis

THE ASSESSMENT PROGRAM AT WASHINGTON UNIVERSITY Libraries is actively building a culture of assessment, where decisions are based on facts, research, and analysis, and where services are planned and delivered in ways that maximize positive outcomes and impacts for customers and stakeholders.[1] The model of a volunteer Assessment Team led by a full-time assessment coordinator provides a flexible framework for cultivating staff knowledge of assessment and facilitating participation on projects, while keeping the emphasis where it belongs—on listening to and supporting library users.

Washington University (not to be confused with the University of Washington) was founded in St. Louis, Missouri, as a private, independent institution of higher learning in 1853. As a medium-sized research and teaching institution, the university serves approximately 12,000 full-time students and employs roughly 3,415 full-time and adjunct faculty. The Danforth Campus is the academic home to the majority of the university's undergraduate, graduate, and professional students, and the site of ten of Washington University's twelve libraries. The Olin Library serves as the university's main library and is located in the center of the Danforth Campus, anchoring the library system.

In the past ten years there has been a gradual shift in academic libraries from concentrating on input and output measures to viewing assessment as a vital component of a customer-centered library. The intent of this chapter is to explain how this evolution occurred at Washington University Libraries, and the impact it produced. A chronology of how the libraries' assessment activities developed forms the foundation of the chapter. This is followed by a look at the role of the assessment coordinator and the purpose and structure of the Assessment Team. The issue of library staff buy-in is addressed next, followed by highlights of key projects and activities and how they impacted both the libraries and users. An analysis of assessment as a transformative process is then provided and the chapter concludes with reflections on program sustainability in a very rapidly changing library and educational environment.

A Brief Chronology of Assessment at Washington University Libraries

Before the establishment of an assessment program in 2006, there was a steady stream of spontaneous assessment activities within the Washington University Libraries. These activities included tracking data for submission to the Association of Research Libraries, collecting data to understand use of the libraries' collections for both acquisitions and space management, and gathering data to understand library space usage. Other projects focused on interacting with users to improve the libraries' customer service and instruction, and collecting information to help improve library workflow and time management. Projects supporting the accreditation needs for several of the university's academic programs were also completed.

With the exception of the submission of ARL statistics, most activity was short-term and contained within the "silos" of individual library units. Levels of analysis were dependent upon the time available, the skills of the librarians involved, and who was making the decisions. Before the implementation of the libraries' intranet in December 2008, data and analyses were generally stored within the offices and computers of the manager who led the assessment effort. This in turn constrained any future sharing and analysis.

In 2003 Washington University Libraries appointed an associate dean for organizational development. She was quickly charged with implementing a LibQUAL survey to solicit, track, understand, and act upon users' opinions of service quality. The survey was distributed to all faculty and students in the spring of 2004, and the results became the springboard for further assessment projects, including faculty interviews and graduate student focus groups. Following the 2004 LibQUAL survey, the associate dean then asked the library staff for volunteers to work on an Assessment Task Force. Nine highly motivated volunteers responded and work began immediately to systematically scan the organization and identify ongoing assessment activities which could be modified or eliminated. A number of projects were discontinued or revised to be more relevant to current decision making. The key message of this project was that staff had permission to revisit data collection and discontinue the gathering of data that was no longer cost-effective.

The Washington University Libraries was one of the first twenty-four libraries to participate in the Association of Research Libraries project "Making Library Assessment Work: Practical Approaches for Developing and Sustaining Effective Assessment." ARL's visiting program officers conducted an evaluation of the Washington University Libraries' assessment program in 2006 and met with the libraries' Assessment Task Force to discuss a wide range of assessment and measurement-related issues. The project's final report offered seven suggestions and options for moving assessment forward.[2] These suggestions included (1) establish practices and procedures for coordinating assessment, including designation of an assessment coordinator; (2) maintain and enhance the libraries' usability experience; (3) help the libraries' staff to understand their role in the assessment process; (4) conduct a service quality survey such as LibQUAL on a three-year cycle; (5) use assessment to enhance understanding of and support for the university enterprise; (6) use multiple methods to assess digital library programs and initiatives; and (7) examine and evaluate statistics kept by the Washington University Libraries.

The ARL program officers noted that the libraries' 2005–2008 Strategic Plan identified assessment as an area of strategic focus. This was an opportunity for the Assessment Task Force to raise the visibility of assessment within the organization and work with library units to develop realistic assessment and evaluation measures. The program officers also highlighted a number of interests and abilities important to the recommended coordinator position, including an interest in assessment and a commitment to the library as a customer-centered enterprise. This individual would need a broad perspective on issues that affect academic libraries and higher education, and an understanding of the value of assessment in improving library services. Skill summarizing and presenting results effectively to diverse audiences was also required, along with an ability to work effectively with staff, managers, and administrators throughout the organization. An effective assessment coordinator would serve as a program spokesperson and leader, and would not simply be a "doer" of assessment activities. This individual would advocate for assessment, serve as a resource person, know best practices, and promote understanding of assessment to the organization. The coordinator should also be positive and supportive and collegial rather than coercive in style.

To help library staff understand their role in the assessment process, the program officers noted that connecting assessment to positive outcomes was important to build support among library staff as well as showing how the libraries add value to the academic and research enterprise. To accomplish this, the libraries needed to raise the knowledge base of librarians in such areas as research methodology and data analysis. The libraries also needed to build support for assessment through effective communication and appropriate training.

In 2006, the libraries used these recommendations with others in the report to fuel the development of a formal assessment program. The Assessment Task Force was replaced with a standing Assessment Team and the associate dean for organizational development was initially designated as the point person for all assessment activities. An assessment coordinator was appointed in September 2008 by "repurposing" a position from the Business Library. The program was further developed by changing the status of the libraries' Usability Team from an ad hoc committee to a standing subgroup of the Assessment Team.

The concept that assessment is everyone's job has been an important ingredient in mainstreaming the libraries' assessment program. To make assessment accessible to all levels of the organization, the libraries offers various seminars and training opportunities to all staff members, with one to three classes covering such topics as outcomes assessment, survey building/analysis, and project management skills each semester.

Roles of the Assessment Coordinator and the Assessment Team

Assigning a full-time assessment coordinator was an important step in moving assessment forward at the Washington University Libraries. The assessment coordinator chairs the Assessment Team and serves as an internal consultant to library staff. The coordinator is responsible for leading the planning and assessment of library programs and services; consulting with library leaders and staff on assessment needs and methods; collecting and analyzing data and preparing reports and presentations; providing assistance to others who are collecting and analyzing both quantitative and qualitative data; training staff in research methods; and representing the assessment point of view on committees/task forces.

In 2008, the assessment coordinator met with library service managers to identify areas where data was needed to make effective management decisions. This initiated a dialogue focused on benchmarking levels of service in all areas of the libraries. The coordinator established the identification of new ways of collecting, analyzing, and presenting data as a priority and led the design, implementation, and delivery of training on assessment techniques.

From the libraries' initial planning stages for an assessment program, through the development of training and a system for coaching library staff, the Assessment Team has been empowered to try different approaches and investigate what works. The team's first challenge following its appointment in 2006 was to define its role and value for the organization. The team developed six questions to guide its planning process: (1) who should be a member of the Assessment Team? (2) how would team members receive training and train library staff? (3) what roles should team members play? (4) how would the team decide what projects to support? (5) how should the team communicate its activities and results? and (6) how will library staff ask the team for help?

To address who should be on the Assessment Team, members agreed that it was important to have an inclusive and cross-sectional representation of staff with differing levels of authority and experience, and from various units, functions, and physical locations. The team currently consists of ten members who rotate off every one and a half to two years. While each member is a volunteer, as team members have cycled off over the years, some effort has been made to maintain cross-sectional representation by extending invitations to individuals to join the team, rather than making an open call.

The team decided to build a hub of knowledge for the libraries to bridge the organization's assessment skill gaps and related training needs. (See figure 11.1.) Each hub was established as an Assessment Team subgroup, with three to four members from both the Assessment Team and the broader library staff dedicated to becoming subject matter experts for the hub topic. Hub concentrations include metrics and statistics; outcomes assessment; surveys, focus groups, and interviews; user insights and feedback; and usability testing. The subgroups continue to be invaluable in allowing the Assessment Team to complete a steady stream of projects. The subgroups initially trained other members of the Assessment Team on issues, methodologies, and techniques related to their hub and then offered training as appropriate to all library staff. An introduction to surveys class, for instance, was offered in 2007 and 2008, with a more advanced class in 2009. An outcomes assessment class was also delivered in 2009, and project management workshops were delivered in 2011. Subgroups of the Assessment Team, however, are always open to all library staff with permission of their supervisor.

When the Assessment Team launched in 2006, few staff librarians had experience leading focus groups, writing surveys, or running interviews. No one had experience with usability testing. It quickly became clear that team member's roles would depend on the project and that these roles would likely change over time. Each project required a fair amount of "figuring it out as we go along." We found that usability testing, for example, was easiest for the assessment program to address with a trained pool of staff that could serve as moderators or note takers. As more and more projects were successfully

FIGURE 11.1

The Washington University Libraries' Assessment Team's Hubs of Knowledge

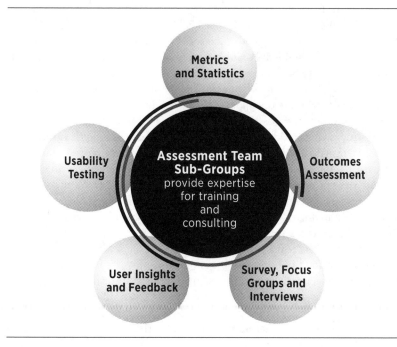

completed, the team members shifted from a coaching role to a consulting role. By 2011 it was not unusual for assessment team members to shift from coaching to providing advice on choosing an appropriate method of assessment, to providing suggestions for how to approach the analysis portion of a project.

The team established priorities for selecting appropriate projects and activities for assessment based on potential user impact. A service quality survey and usability testing on the catalog search box, for example, were identified as having high impact, and consequently become high-priority projects. The need to preserve survey equity is also an important consideration in determining a project's scope and viability. The team delayed the distribution of several surveys because the timing would have bombarded users with too many requests for feedback. A faculty survey on data management originally planned for the fall semester of 2010, for example, was deferred until late January 2011 because plans were in place to distribute a service quality survey at the same time. Another consideration for selecting projects is the effort required in relation to expected outcomes. While it is rare for the

Assessment Team to turn down a project, it is not unusual to recommend trading one assessment tool or methodology for another that might be more cost-effective.

Each month the Assessment Team presents an Assessment Minute at a meeting the libraries' dean holds for all library staff. This has proved to be the single most effective forum for communicating the team's activities and results. The team uses the Assessment Minute to spotlight hot projects and provide teachable moments. For one monthly meeting, staff arrived to find bagels, cream cheese, orange juice, and donuts with calorie counts prominently displayed. The message of the Assessment Minute for that month was that calorie counting is an example of how everyone assesses, all the time. Awareness of data, such as calorie counts, helps you to make better decisions. To make the Assessment Team more transparent to staff, a website was established on the library intranet to post assessment announcements, results, and provide links to other useful websites. In addition, a LibGuide was launched in 2011 to make the libraries' assessment activities more visible to users (http://libguides.wustl.edu/assessment). This website not only shares the results of assessment activities with library users, but also provides a spot for users to volunteer to help with future projects or answer quick polls. The LibGuide also provides the libraries' staff the means to share their activities with a growing community of assessment practitioners.

The Assessment Team developed a multistep process to help library staff ask for help with assessment activities and handle requests for support. First the librarian or staff member (client) seeking assistance must go to the libraries' intranet site and complete an Assessment Activity Form. This form is well advertised and available in several highly visible locations. The assessment coordinator then receives the form as an e-mail alert and after a quick evaluation, assigns the request to an appropriate member of the assessment team. This assignment is based on the skill set most likely needed, such as expertise with surveys or usability studies. The Assessment Team member then meets with the client to help the client to identify the goals, time lines, and most suitable assessment tools for the project. If it is determined that the Assessment Team member's expertise is not a good fit for the project, a handoff to the team member who can best help the client will be arranged. A project team leader is then established. The team leader may be the client, if the client possesses project management expertise. If this is the case, the Assessment Team member will remain involved in the project, functioning as a sounding board during the execution phase. The team member may also help to guide the client through the analysis and reporting stage of the project, developing recommendations for change or further assessment. When a project is completed, final documents and data are collected and stored in the Assessment Project Archive folder on the libraries' intranet.

Securing Staff Support for Library Assessment Activities

Between 2009 and 2010, the number of assessment requests rose steadily. By late 2010 over 88 percent of the libraries' staff had been directly involved in an assessment project, and over 2,500 library users had participated in surveys, focus groups, interviews, or usability testing. Staff support for assessment projects and activities grew gradually over time, as the program overcame a variety of challenges. Four particular challenges central to the acceptance of assessment by the libraries' staff included establishing credibility for the program, converting the skeptical, expanding the libraries' pool of assessment talent, and making assessment enjoyable.

The Assessment Team has been fortunate to have strong and visible support from the libraries' administration for its activities. The team's credibility was established through participation in high-profile projects that delivered results that fueled planning, decision making, and change. The team has also demonstrated a willingness to assess its own activities and admit what has and has not worked, modeling behavior for the entire library organization.

To convert the skeptical, the team consciously recruited individuals who were shying away from the libraries' assessment program for short-term projects with personal relevance. Team members also worked to assign skeptics tasks that showcased their strengths. For instance, a reticent cataloger who might be uncomfortable facilitating a focus group could be eased into the process as a note taker in a usability session. Skeptics who are visibly aligned with a successful project tend to be less vocal in their overall critique of the program.

While training sessions expanded the libraries' pool of talent, turnover on the Assessment Team itself has provided a growing number of skilled staff members who can participate on future projects. Each project "graduates" more experienced assessors, who in turn become candidates for future projects. While assessment is often not equated with fun, making it enjoyable pays enormous dividends. Participation on an assessment project should never be a pain or imposition. Staff work schedules should be respected, so that no one is required to do more than their share, or feel that their core responsibilities are compromised. Tasks are assigned to showcase the talents of library staff, wherever possible, and recognition is frequent.

While participation rates suggest strong support for the libraries assessment program, there is also compelling anecdotal evidence that indicates progress in establishing a culture of assessment is being made. It is not unusual to hear someone comment in a committee meeting "Do we know what students are doing?" or "Has anyone talked to faculty about this?" Some areas of observation that warrant further investigation pertain to the impact of assessment activities on the speed and quality of decision making. Based

DEVELOPING A LIBRARY ASSESSMENT PROGRAM AT WASHINGTON UNIVERSITY / 163

on personal observation alone, with the growth in assessment activities, there seem to be fewer decisions based solely on internal consensus. Decisions are now informed with direct input from students and faculty. Having more user evidence available also appears to facilitate decision making at lower levels of the organization, which provides for a more responsive and agile operation.

The most energizing assessment activities are those with a large impact on the way faculty and students interact with the library. In 2004 and 2007 the Libraries used LibQUAL to collect feedback from users on the quality of the libraries' services and analyze the libraries' performance in relation to a variety of peer institutions. In 2010 a decision was made to develop a local, customized survey instrument to capture detail unique to the Washington University environment. The Service Quality Survey resulted, continuing the libraries' ongoing dialogue with users concerning their needs and expectations for the libraries.

Results from the 2010 Service Quality Survey identified a number of distinct areas of user concern, such as improving Wi-Fi coverage, increasing the hours the libraries are open, providing more collaborative work areas, and resolving issues with the catalog interface. The libraries responded quickly with additional assessment activities aimed at clarifying the issues that surfaced and identifying possible solutions. The libraries' IT organization, for instance, worked throughout the summer of 2011 to identify weak spots in the Libraries' Wi-Fi map. The libraries installed seventeen new wireless access points as a result of this project and upgraded nineteen existing wireless access points.

The need for extended hours of operation continues to be one of the most repeated comments among students. After analyzing the number of survey comments related to hours, a team was formed to address student concerns. A survey of library directors at peer institutions confirmed that many have opened their libraries around the clock in response to similar demands on their campuses. The library hours team recommended that the Washington University Libraries remain open 24 hours a day on four days of the week, with a 24 hours-a-day, seven days-a-week schedule during reading and exam time. The libraries is currently exploring funding options for this recommendation, and expects to trial these hours within the next year. In the interim, efforts were made to improve communication of the libraries' current hours and late night availability via its website.

Since today's students spend more time on team projects and group study, it was not surprising that students answering the survey made it clear that they desired more collaborative study space. During peak study times in the semester, students particularly have difficulty finding enough collaborative space for study. Space planning is a continuing process for the libraries, particularly in its main Olin Library facility. While the migration from print to electronic resources has opened space throughout the Olin Library, teams are currently working on repurposing this space by adding study tables, providing collaborative table configurations with supporting media, and improving lighting for late night study.

The libraries added a new discovery layer to its catalog in the fall of 2011. Initial feedback revealed that faculty and students prefer to go directly to the libraries' classic or underlying catalog, without having to sift through the new discovery layer. Additional feedback from subject librarians indicated that researchers needed faster, more direct "known item" searching. The configuration of the search box on the libraries' website was improved as a result and all catalog options are now displayed together. In addition, the space at the bottom of the search box now describes what is included in each type of catalog to help users decide which level to choose.

While formal projects like the Service Quality Survey or evaluating discovery catalog options surface about once a year, most library assessment projects are relatively short and action-focused. In 2009, we made a conscious effort to balance the value of collecting information against the cost of gathering it. We began a number of Assessment Lite projects, focusing on quick and simple testing approaches intended to reduce interruption to the normal flow of a student's day. Assessment Lite projects are designed to gather immediately actionable data. One example of this approach was positioning a library staffer and a laptop in the library lobby during class changes to check which of two navigation styles students preferred. For another project, whiteboards were scattered throughout the main library building. Each board gathered candid comments regarding software options for the libraries. A third project involved positioning library staff in the Student Union during lunch hours to interact with students on the topic of upcoming library technology classes.

Assessment and Transformative Change

One of the most notable impacts of the assessment program at the Washington University Libraries is that it has served as a catalyst for change—both in the way we interact with users, and the decisions we make on their behalf. One interesting approach to evaluating the success of the libraries' assessment program is to borrow criteria from a business context. In his article "Why Transformation Efforts Fail," Harvard Business School Professor John P. Kotter suggests eight steps to transforming an organization.[3] Considering the Washington University Libraries assessment program in light of these criteria offers some interesting insights into how the libraries transformed its culture into a culture of assessment.

Kotter cites *establishing a sense of urgency* as the first step for transforming an organization. In the case of the libraries, participating in the ARL project

"Making Library Assessment Work: Practical Approaches" was critical in build-ing a sense that assessment was vital to our role as a user-centric, relevant academic library. Additionally, the vice-chancellor for scholarly resources and dean of university libraries is a strong proponent of using data for decision making, interlibrary cooperation, and collaboration. As a result, the libraries' staff heard loud and clear that assessment was part of the libraries' future. It was needed for understanding our users, adapting our services, and demon-strating our value. This sense of urgency was reinforced by the appointment of an assessment coordinator in 2008.

The second step is *forming a powerful guiding coalition*. At Washington University Libraries we are fortunate to have the full support of the libraries' administration. The presence of two associate deans on the Assessment Team since it formed—the associate dean for organizational development and the associate dean of access, bibliographic, and information services—has meant that our guiding coalition was knowledgeable and well positioned for making decisions that impacted the entire organization. Having the associate dean of access involved also gave the team clout, particularly with staff that interact directly with users. This allowed us to assess customer service and outreach issues more quickly. After two years, the associate dean of access cycled off the team, but remains a continued source of guidance and support for assessment activities.

The third step for transforming an organization is *creating a vision*. The Assessment Team faced the challenge of defining how assessment functions within the organization. An important part of this challenge was to look at the libraries' strategic plan to identify how assessment could support its larger mission. At the same time, the Assessment Team also developed a mission to build a culture of assessment in the twelve libraries, where decisions are based on facts, research, and analysis, and where services are planned and deliv-ered in ways that maximize positive outcomes and impacts for customers and stakeholders. An important part of creating the vision was articulating core beliefs, which linked the assessment program to other important initiatives in the library. The assessment program recognizes the importance of users in both internal and external contexts. In a decentralized organization, we are customers to one another. The program also supports the position that assess-ment is everyone's responsibility and that insight comes from all levels and leads to continuous improvement in services. Balancing the costs of acquiring information with the value of the knowledge gained is an important element of the program.

The fourth step requires us to *communicate the vision*. The assessment program plans were shared in a variety of ways. The monthly dean's meet-ings continue to be an important outlet for information on assessment goals and direction, basic concepts of assessment, and success stories. An intra-net site was dedicated to assessment activities and archives. Most recently a LibGuide was added to the libraries' website to make program information available to faculty and students as well as library staff (www.libguide.wustl .edu/assessment).

Empowering others to act on the vision is the fifth step for transforming an organization. By late 2010 over 88 percent of library staff had been directly involved in surveys, focus groups, interviews, or usability testing projects. It was not difficult to generate interest in assessment projects. Most library professionals were eager to use the tools to better understand and connect with users. By providing peer-level assistance and easy access to Assessment Team members through the Assessment Activity Form, library staff members were encouraged to take on more projects than they would normally be able to handle on their own. Another important aspect of empowerment flowed from communicating that assessment is a mindset as well as a skill set. Cues that this mindset is now in operation within the libraries include the development of peer review in library instruction and the requirement for articulation of outcomes in the librarian promotion process. Another important message was that assessment is everyone's responsibility, at all levels. The Assessment Team acts as the hub of knowledge, not the sole practitioners for the libraries' assessment activities.

Kotter's sixth step identifies the need to *plan for and create short-term wins*. The Assessment Team initially rallied around high-impact, high-visibility projects like the LibQUAL surveys and the website usability efforts. Over time, impact increased when the team showcased successes that originated within the organization, such as the survey of faculty to determine their data management behaviors and needs, or the focus groups to evaluate space planning in the Olin Library. In 2008 the libraries developed a reward/incentive program called the AAA Awards (All About Attitude). This program was aimed at recognizing excellent customer service. Bookstore gift cards of $25 were awarded to the four top submissions, three times per year. This program recognized many assessment efforts related to understanding user needs and behaviors in order to deliver better service.

After some short-term wins are realized, Kotter suggests the next step to transform an organization is to *consolidate improvements and produce still more change*. Credibility for the libraries' assessment efforts was built on large projects that impacted the entire organization. Usability testing of the libraries' main web page, for instance, triggered a redesign of the look, feel, and navigation of the entire libraries' website. This in turn led to the formation of a web team to manage the site utilizing a more user-centric model.

The final step for transforming an organization is *institutionalizing new approaches*. "The way we do things around here" at the Washington University Libraries has indeed changed. We collect less data, and analyze the information that we do gather in more meaningful ways. As Douglas Cook expressed it, "Doing research is only part of the process. Reporting the research is only part of the process. It is necessary to close the loop by using research conclusions to initiate changes in the library. Furthermore, those interventions need to be evaluated to see if they do, in fact, improve the situation."[4] The libraries' assessment program has been effective in using research to trigger changes, but more work needs to be done to institutionalize the final step of confirming outcomes. We have succeeded in changing the way library staff think about and interact with users. Our emphasis has shifted from being a reactive library that waits for a complaint to being a proactive library that understands what users are thinking, how they do their work, and how we can adapt our service to those needs.

Conclusion

The assessment program at Washington University Libraries continues to evolve. The role of the Assessment Team has shifted from frequent training and consulting to acting as a sounding board for projects, providing updated training agendas, and emphasizing data analysis. The role of the assessment coordinator position has expanded as well, with the coordinator working to build connections with peer groups within the university as well as to contribute to an active learning community of practitioners.

Subgroups of the Assessment Team continue to change to reflect the hubs, or areas of knowledge that need emphasis. The groups for Culture of Assessment and Outcomes Assessment were established to focus the libraries' knowledge on these topics. As we internalized the issues, these groups were disbanded, on the argument that these issues were now implicitly covered in all other assessment activities. The User Experience subgroup grew out of a library planning team focused on user feedback. The Metrics and Statistics subgroup expanded to incorporate the ARL statistics submission, which was previously handled by library administration.

While the assessment program at the Washington University Libraries has progressed considerably, there are still a number of opportunities on the horizon. Constructing a toolkit of research analysis skills for subject librarians—both qualitative and quantitative—remains a priority. Looking for new ways to align our metrics and share data with the larger university organization is another area that deserves further attention.

In 2012 the leadership of the Libraries experienced significant change with the retirement of the dean and two associate deans. Work to develop a vision that will make the libraries more responsive and relevant to academic life at Washington University is in progress. Each unit within the libraries is currently involved in articulating its respective roles, responsibilities, and plans for the future. The assessment program has an integral role to play in bridging this transition, providing data and analysis to help the new leadership understand and manage this new environment.

The culture of assessment at Washington University Libraries continues to grow. Using the ARL program officer's visit as a springboard, the libraries developed a model assessment infrastructure that is well suited to our libraries' staff levels and decentralized structure. Our combination of a volunteer Assessment Team led by a full-time assessment coordinator provides a flexible framework for increasing staff knowledge and participation on projects, while keeping the emphasis where it belongs, on listening to and supporting library users.

NOTES

1. Amos Lakos, Shelley Phipps, and Betsy Wilson, "Defining a Culture of Assessment," www.lib.uwaterloo.ca/~aalakos/Assessment%20Plus/CulAssessToolkit/Assessdef3.doc. The full definition used was: "A Culture of Assessment is an organizational environment in which decisions are based on facts, research and analysis, and where services are planned and delivered in ways which maximize positive outcomes and impacts for customers and stakeholders. A culture of assessment exists in organizations where staff care to know what results they produce and how those results relate to structures and systems support behavior that is performance and learning focused."

2. Steve Hiller and James Self, "Washington University Libraries Evaluation and Suggestions for Effective and Sustainable Assessment," report, visiting program officers (Association of Research Libraries, July 2006), 3.

3. John P. Kotter, "Why Transformation Efforts Fail," *Harvard Business Review* (March-April 1995): 59–67.

4. Douglas Cook, "The Recursive Cycle of Qualitative Action Research," in *Using Quantitative Methods in Action Research: How Librarians Can Get to the Why of Data,* ed. Douglas Cook et al. (Association of College and Research Libraries, 2011), 21.

Contributors

Terriruth Carrier is new to higher education and library science. She joined Syracuse University Library in 2008 as a project manager after spending thirty years helping businesses become more productive and efficient using Six Sigma and process improvement techniques and methodologies. She is now the director of program management at the libraries. Carrier has a BS in industrial engineering and operations research and an MS in engineering administration, both from Syracuse University.

Mary-Deirdre Coraggio has worked in public, academic, and technical libraries throughout her career. She is currently director of the Information Services Office at the National Institute of Standards and Technology (NIST). In this role, she directs the NIST Research Library, the NIST Museum and History Program, and the NIST Electronic Information Program. Coraggio attained her MLIS from Pratt Institute. She is the former head of the Technical Library Division for the Naval Warfare Center Weapons Division. She is an active lecturer, educator, and author.

Kate Davis was recently named the assistant director for collections and digital preservation at Scholars Portal, a division of the Ontario Council of University Libraries (OCUL). Prior to this assignment, she was the coordinator of the Scholars Portal Ebooks project. Davis earned an MLS in 2006 and an MA in Russian and East European studies in 2003, both from the University of Toronto. She has worked as a librarian with Scholars Portal since 2006, providing support to OCUL libraries for various Scholars Portal services.

Kymberly Anne Goodson is a decision support analyst for the University of California, San Diego (UCSD) Libraries. Her primary responsibilities include investigating the library user experience; developing and implementing services to meet user needs; conducting user and usability studies; and collecting and analyzing data and other information to support effective library management decision making. She is currently developing a New Learning Spaces program for the UCSD Libraries. Goodson earned her MLIS in 1998 from the University of Illinois at Urbana-Champaign. She has published in *PS: Political Science & Politics*, the *Journal of Access Services*, and the *Journal of Interlibrary Loan, Document Delivery, and Electronic Reserve*.

Steve Hiller is director of planning and assessment at the University of Washington Libraries. Prior to assuming this position in 2006, he had been head of science libraries and library assessment coordinator. Hiller has been active in the library assessment community for twenty years, presenting and publishing widely on assessment-related topics. He also serves as an assessment consultant and is co-chair of the Library Assessment Conference, which has been held biennially since 2006. His current interests include user needs assessment, organizational performance metrics, and developing organizational capacity for assessment.

Laurel Ann Littrell is the director of library planning and assessment at Kansas State University Libraries. Her previous positions at Kansas State include head of the General Information Services Department, interim assistant dean for Public Services, chair of Social Sciences/Humanities Libraries, and humanities reference librarian. Littrell is an active member on university committees and councils related to assessment, technology, planning, and mentoring. She received her MLS from Emporia State University. She also earned a BM and an MM degree in music theory/composition from Kansas State University and a DMA from the Conservatory of Music at the University of Missouri–Kansas City.

Susan Makar is a librarian and laboratory liaison in the Electronic Information and Publications Program at the National Institute of Standards and

Technology (NIST), an agency of the U.S. Department of Commerce. As the liaison to the Material Measurement Laboratory and the NIST Program Coordination Office, Makar performs impact analyses and publication assessments for NIST scientists, technical staff, and management. She began her library career as a reference librarian at Texas Tech University Libraries, where she later served as coordinator of computer-assisted search services. Makar has also served as a science reference librarian at Georgetown University Libraries. She earned her MLIS from the University of Iowa.

Lucretia McCulley is currently director of outreach services at Boatwright Memorial Library, University of Richmond, Virginia. McCulley provides administrative oversight for the Outreach Services Division, which includes instruction and information services; customer service; and stacks, building, and interlibrary loan services. Other areas of responsibility include assessment, marketing, public relations, and staff development. McCulley serves as the liaison librarian for the Jepson School of Leadership Studies and the Women, Gender and Sexuality Studies Program. She received a BA in history from Salem College and an MSLS from the University of Tennessee. She is currently a consulting editor for the SAGE Reference handbook series on various leadership topics, including *Gender and Women's Leadership: A Reference Handbook* and *Political and Civic Leadership: A Reference Handbook.*

Carol Mollman, following a career in the business sector and as an adjunct professor in business communications at Aurora University, transitioned into academic librarianship as associate director of the Kopolow Business Library at Washington University in St. Louis. She is currently assessment coordinator for the Washington University Libraries. Mollman earned an MBA from Columbia University and an MLIS from the University of Kentucky. She frequently presents on assessment and business-related topics. She also currently serves on the Library Advisory Board of the Federal Reserve Bank of St. Louis.

Sarah Anne Murphy has held numerous positions at the Ohio State University Libraries since 1999. She is currently coordinator of assessment there. Murphy earned an MLS degree from Kent State University in 2000 and an MBA from Ohio State's Fisher College of Business in 2008. She is the author of *The Librarian as Information Consultant* (2011) and has published papers on Lean Six Sigma, mentoring, and issues related to veterinary medicine libraries in *College & Research Libraries,* the *Journal of Academic Librarianship,* and the *Journal of the Medical Library Association.*

Mylene Ouimette is a research librarian and laboratory liaison in the Research Library and Information Group at the National Institute of Standards and

Technology (NIST). Ouimette conducts impact analyses, market and industry research, and other assessment studies for scientists and managers in the NIST Physical Measurement Laboratory (PML). She also represents and articulates the PML's needs in all matters related to the NIST Research Library's collections and services. Ouimette has master degrees in both engineering and library science from the University of Maryland.

Chestalene Pintozzi has held several positions at the University of Arizona (UA) Libraries since 1989. She is currently director of project management and assessment. Pintozzi has served on the UA Libraries' Information Resources Council and the Strategic Long Range Planning Team and on the University of Arizona's Strategic Planning and Budget Advisory Committee. Prior to her tenure at the UA Libraries, Pintozzi was the geology librarian at the University of Texas at Austin. Pintozzi earned her MLIS from the University of Texas at Austin in 1982. She has published in *Library Administration & Management* and presented at the American Library Association's Annual Conferences.

Barbara P. Silcox is program manager for the Electronic Information and Publications Program at the National Institute of Standards and Technology (NIST), an agency of the U.S. Department of Commerce. Silcox has enjoyed a career in a variety of library and information settings, including two years with the Baldrige National Quality Program at NIST where she conducted marketing and outreach activities and contributed to the rewriting of the 2000 Education Criteria for Performance Excellence. Silcox earned her MLS from the University of Maryland. She has published papers and presented on topics related to organizational performance assessment.

Daniel Suchy served as a user services technology analyst at the University of California, San Diego Libraries until 2012, when he became manager of the UC San Diego Instructional Web Development Center. As user services technology analyst, Suchy experimented with a broad range of technologies to improve the library user experience. In his new role, Suchy is working to identify and implement a technical strategy for online course delivery and faculty support. He also oversees the campus's course podcast program and works toward making it and other online instruction offerings more accessible to those with disabilities. Suchy received both an MIS and an MLS from Indiana University. His recent publications have appeared in *Code4Lib Journal* and *D-Lib Magazine*.

Dana Thomas has been a librarian at Ryerson University Library and Archives since 2005, after earning her MIS degree from the University of Toronto's iSchool. At Ryerson, Thomas has worked in the areas of serials, electronic resources, and collection management and evaluation. She is currently the evaluation and assessment librarian at Ryerson and chairs the Evaluation and Assessment Committee for the Ontario Council of University Libraries (OCUL). From 2010 to 2011, Thomas was seconded to the Scholars Portal project within OCUL to establish an evaluation and assessment for the consortium. Thomas has presented at numerous Canadian and international conferences and with Ophelia Cheung and Susan Patrick has coauthored the book *New Approaches to E-Reserve: Linking, Sharing and Streaming* (2010).

Emily Thornton has worked in the administration office of the Emory University Libraries for nearly five years. After earning a BA in anthropology from Emory University, she enrolled in the SLIS program at the University of South Carolina. Thornton completed her MLIS degree in 2012. Her interests include the user experience and digital librarianship in the field of academic libraries.

Nancy B. Turner is librarian and research and assessment analyst at Syracuse University Library. In this role she collects and analyzes qualitative and quantitative data to understand changing user needs for library resources, services, and facilities. Turner earned an MLIS from Clark Atlanta University, an MA in social sciences from the University of Chicago, and a BA in anthropology from the University of Pennsylvania. Her research interests include the use of anthropological methods in understanding the culture of libraries and their users; information-seeking behavior and the usability of web interfaces; and the organization of data for library assessment.

Xuemao Wang is dean and university librarian at the University of Cincinnati, effective August 31, 2012. He was most recently the associate vice provost for the Emory University Libraries, where he provided oversight for the day-to-day operations of the libraries and directly supervised the libraries' Administration Division, Content Division, and Services Division. Wang currently serves as chair of the IFLA Knowledge Management section. He has a strong interest and background in information technology management and global librarianship and has worked to strengthen ties between American and Chinese libraries. Wang earned an MLS from Kutztown University of Pennsylvania, an MLIS from the University of South Carolina, and an MBA from Hofstra University. He has authored several papers and book chapters, and is regularly invited to give international keynote presentations.

Lynda S. White has worked at the University of Virginia Library since 1977, holding various positions in the Fiske Kimball Fine Arts Library and in Management Information Services. She received an MS in library science from the University of North Carolina in 1972 and an MA in art history from the University of Virginia in 1979. White has been on the executive boards of both the Visual Resources Association and the Art Libraries Society. She has published several articles in both art and library journals; the *ArtMARC Sourcebook: Cataloging Art, Architecture, and Their Visual Images* (1998); and with Stephanie Wright, an ARL SPEC Kit on *Library Assessment* (2007).

Stephanie Wright earned her MLIS from the University of Washington in 2001. After working as a computing trainer for the Bill & Melinda Gates Foundation, she returned to the University of Washington Libraries as a science librarian. In 2006 Wright became management information librarian in the Libraries Office of Assessment and Planning. She has helped to coordinate multiple library user surveys, managed collection of various library statistics, served on the conference planning team for the 2008 Library Assessment Conference, and coauthored an ARL SPEC Kit on Library Assessment. Wright was appointed the data services coordinator for the University of Washington Libraries in 2010.

Index